Garden Details

ACCENTS, ORNAMENTS, AND FINISHING TOUCHES FOR THE GARDEN

Garden Details

ACCENTS, ORNAMENTS, AND
FINISHING TOUCHES FOR THE GARDEN

WARREN SCHULTZ • CAROL SPIER

MetroBooks

MetroBooks

An imprint of Friedman/Fairfax Publishers

Library of Congress Cataloging-in-Publication Data

Schultz, Warren.
     Garden details : accents, ornaments, and finishing touches for your garden / Warren Schultz, Carol Spier.
        p.   cm.
     Includes bibliographical references (p.   ) and index.
     ISBN 1-56799-635-3
     1. Garden ornaments and furniture. 2. Garden structures.
3. Plants, potted. 4. Garden ornaments and furniture--Pictorial works. 5. Garden structures--Pictorial works. 6. Plants, potted--Pictorial works. I. Spier, Carol. II. Title
     SB473.5.S364   1998
     717--dc21   97-30402

Editors: Susan Lauzau, Stephen Slaybaugh, Kelly Matthews
Art Directors: Kevin Ullrich, Jeff Batzli, Lynne Yeamans
Designers: Charles Donahue, Tanya Ross-Hughes, Stan Stanski, Phillip Travisano
Photography Director: Christopher C. Bain
Photography Editors: Susan Mettler, Colleen Branigan, Samantha Larrance, Amy Talluto

Color separations by Fine Arts Repro House Co., Ltd.
Printed in China by Leefung-Asco Printers Ltd.

For bulk purchases and special sales, please contact:
Friedman/Fairfax Publishers
Attention: Sales Department
15 West 26th Street
New York, New York 10010
212/685-6610 FAX 212/685-1307

Visit our website:
http://www.metrobooks.com

Table of Contents

Introduction

USING ORNAMENTS TO ENHANCE
GARDEN STYLE   6

INTRODUCTION
Using Ornaments to Enhance Garden Style

*S*ome of the finest gardens make wonderful impressions based purely on the merit of skillful planting. Some—but really few indeed. Of course a handsome garden turns on plants selected with care, and well grown and maintained. That said, there are other factors that are terribly important to a successful result. Chief among these is garden design. When the essential structure (what some people call "the bones") of the garden is strong, any number of plant combinations can be used to good effect; it's not so much the particular plants, but the structure of the garden that carries the day. Pots of money can be spent on choice or hard-to-find varieties, but without a well-considered design, it won't be money well spent. Design comes first, and then you plant.

Garden design must be complicated to be impressive, isn't that so? That needn't be the case at all. Simple may be exquisite, and yet not plain, and this is where a garden ornament can be a tremendous help. Your garden may be formal or informal, severe or romantic, tailored or blowsy, and the type of garden you are working toward will help determine the overall design scheme. The general look you want is usually a decision to settle right off the bat when a new garden is in the making. But what if you are looking to strengthen the design of an existing garden, or are ready to take the next step in designing a new one? Where do you begin to clothe those good garden "bones"? Consider garden ornament.

Architectural features and other garden accents are an excellent way to strengthen design. Walls and fences, benches and garden seats, arbors and gazebos, pools and fountains—all of these are wonderful ways to add design interest. The feature or enhancement you choose to add to your garden may serve a particular function, or it may be essentially decorative, but it offers a wonderful dividend. It acts as a focal point, or an inspiration for design on a more intimate scale. The bottom line? Ornamentation, be it massive or minute, makes for a prettier garden. And using garden ornaments to highlight your property is a good deal easier than you probably think.

Walls and fences offer garden ornamentation on the largest scale. (Sometimes it's difficult to tell where a wall leaves off as an architectural feature and becomes "ornamental," but that isn't necessarily an important distinction.) In any event, walls and fences establish boundaries and define vistas—and they are able to do this not just seasonally, but all year long. In other words, adding a wall or fence to your garden can improve your garden design year-round. Picture rolling lawns sweeping away from a house, sprinkled toward the edge of the property with scattered shrubs or trees. Now add a wall, and those same shrubs or trees pop into focus—they stand out in relief, taking on weight and importance. They look as though you meant them to be where they are. The lawn seems to look softer in contrast to the substance of the wall, too. There is a delicious contrast of texture. A wall can pull the garden picture together. A lush border of many different sorts of flowers, viewed against the uniform background of a garden wall, looks less scattershot than it otherwise might.

Walls and fences are naturally hardworking, too. In addition to creating boundaries, they are frequently the ideal screen for undesirable views. They can not only suggest, but actually create, privacy; the small city garden becomes a peaceful refuge behind sheltering walls, shielded from the frantic urban bustle with its noise and dirt. A retaining wall bands soil in place, a decorative insurance against erosion or a landscaping boon that allows for terracing. A planted wall offers an unusual setting for a garden in miniature, and many an alpine enthusiast has lovingly lodged their tiny rock garden specimens in among the stones of such a wall; other sorts of planted walls function as large-scale containers, bringing refreshing green or splashes of bright color to the situation. Don't forget that walls and fences offer a vertical dimension to the garden, too, supporting plants as diverse as ivy and beans, roses and wisteria. They offer very effective backdrop possibilities, too; walls and fences can be used as foils to highlight the plantings that grow in front of them, making the plants look by contrast fresher and more, well, plantlike.

The choice of material helps determine whether a wall or fence "pops" or blends into the landscape. There may be enormous contrast or sympathy of color or texture. Choose from brick, concrete, stone, rock and mortar, or even adobe, to name a few. And, as you will see in the pages that follow, not all walls are lifeless. Hedges, for example, are walls that grow. The vertical canvas of green offered by a hedge can become a garden showpiece. Hedges notwithstanding, it's unlikely any wall or fence will look "natural" (after all, they are often intended to introduce a note of the man-made into the landscape), but some materials stand out more than others. Bamboo, for example, adds a decidedly exotic note. Metal may look high-tech, high-concept, or high-security, but most likely it won't be unobtrusive. Split-rail fences suggest rusticity, while painted picket fences speak of well-tended domesticity. Brick is a particularly versatile medium, compatible with design schemes that run from colonial to postmodern.

For all their diversity, walls and fences have a look of utility about them. As you might expect, some do indeed serve essential functions, while others just look as though they might. (Really, they are garden accents disguised as enclosures.) Objects used as true garden accents, on the other hand, rarely aspire to the pretension of being essential. The raison d'être of garden accents is to decorate, to stand around and look pretty. Some gardeners use accents as they would jewelry, a little adornment here and there (or a gaudy abundance all about, in the spirit of too much never being enough). Others use them for their magnetic effect, which draws attention to the accents' surroundings rather than to the object itself. Garden accents reflect the taste of the gardener, each piece having been selected

ABOVE: This pretty garden is filled to overflow with plants, but a subtle order is imposed with the addition of a traditional garden bench and a sturdy brick retaining wall. The silvery seat is both accent and resting place, and the wall provides an artful backdrop for plants to drape themselves upon.

ABOVE: This quietly formal corner of the garden makes excellent use of an array of garden ornaments. Potted boxwood, a trough filled with stones, and a medallion-like fountain set into the wall combine in a pleasing show of symmetry that will add beauty to the garden no matter what the season.

from among others, and deliberately set in a specific spot chosen just so. One can always try to disclaim the effect of a planting: the color of the flowers wasn't what you'd expected, or perhaps the summer was so dry the combinations didn't grow together as you'd intended. But beware, no such disclaimers wash when it comes to decorating the garden with objects. Garden accent is self-conscious, and a naturalistic effect isn't usually the aim.

Where walls and fences often wear an air of permanence, garden accents can seem positively transient, as is the case, for example, with statuary of all but the largest proportions. Smallish objects can be carted about on a whim, rather in the fashion of rearranging the furniture indoors. Precisely what can be used as a garden accent? An amazing diversity of objects, some with no seeming relationship to the garden. All objects placed as accents in the garden have two things in common: they all invite attention and none is really necessary. There the similarity stops. Choose your accent for the effect you wish to create. Some are soothing, as in the case of a small, splashing fountain. Some, such as sculpture, might be romantic or starkly contemporary. A birdbath invites wildlife into the garden while adding a vertical line to the picture. A pathway of stone teases the onlooker to explore, while one of brick imposes a civilizing note on its surroundings. Arbors and summer houses, lanterns and sundials, all nominally useful, make memorable garden accents. Topiary, wall plaques, grottoes, and dry stream beds, while they serve no garden function in a narrow sense, highlight their surroundings and contrast the natural with the artificial. And always, placing an object in the garden creates the opportunity to design plantings around that object—your chance to create a unique effect.

Of all garden accents, is any more familiar than the potted plant? It's hard to beat plants in pots and containers for an easy way to bring glorious variety and color to your garden. Unfortunately, it is equally easy to fall into a rut when decorating with potted plants, and that's why it can be refreshing to take a look at what other gardeners dream up. There is much more to decorating with containers than rows of identical pots and saucers. Borrow freely from the scores of ideas and combinations beautifully photographed in these pages. The gardener never has a freer hand in selecting plants than when choosing them for containers, because sun exposure is of primary importance, while hardiness is seldom a concern. Make the most of this advantage, and pot up lots of plants you might not risk putting out in garden beds.

A selection of containers makes a sort of "instant garden" unto itself, one that might take up residence on a patio where not a speck of soil is to be found. This is a "garden" that can be rearranged far more easily than a bed of annuals or an herbaceous border. Pots can be placed around terraces and along walkways. Flanking a doorway, a pair of containers greets the visitor with stately boxwood or amiable primroses. Vegetables, herbs, succulents, bulbs, vines, shrubs, trees, and perennials are candidates every bit as worthy as annuals.

Don't limit your palette of containers to terra-cotta. Let baskets, window boxes, urns, tubs, half barrels, and planters, among many other possibilities, tempt you. In the pages that follow, you can admire old bathtubs, antique milk cans, and even a pair of boots whimsically planted. Let container-grown plants really earn their keep. Formally planted with topiary, they dress up their situation. On a city windowsill, they provide a handy herb garden. And if a plant in the garden fails to live up to expectations, fill that hole with a potted specimen, and no one may suspect that wasn't the bold effect you had in mind all along.

Unforgettable gardens give the impression that someone really spends time there. They are so beautiful that one imagines hours of tranquil bliss spent in their sheltering peace. No one wants to linger in a garden so stiff that it says "Hands off" or "Watch your step and keep moving." You can encourage that welcoming sort of beauty by placing a bench or seat in your garden; the bench will look enticing, and give your garden a sort of established attitude because it assumes there is something worth sitting down to admire in the first place.

In the best tradition of garden ornaments, a seat or bench can be a point of departure for a planting scheme. A rustic chair under a rose-covered arbor, an intimate wrought-iron table and chairs in a leafy bower, a stone bench at the end of a soft-hued peony walk—so many combinations suggest themselves. You may, however, prefer seating that instead blends in with its surroundings, so look to the many unusual suggestions for everything from the discreet to the unabashedly practical.

Wherever you garden, the possibilities for garden ornamentation are vast. You may choose everyday objects, or if you are artistically inclined, you may try your hand at fashioning something on your own. On page 282 you will find a helpful listing of sources for garden furniture, trellises, fencing, and the like, so no matter where you are or what your taste may be, you will be able to find the touches that will make your garden vision become reality.

—Rebecca W. Atwater Briccetti

Part One

GARDEN ACCENTS

INTRODUCTION

From their very beginnings as the pleasure grounds of the ancient Near East, gardens have been artful combinations of living plants and man-made ornaments. Gardens are where human nature and mother nature exist in harmony.

As earthbound representations of paradise, gardens have been adorned through the ages with statues of deities and spirits. Over time, garden accents became more earthly and practical, though no less artful. From the magnificent fountains of Persia to the elaborate steps of Italian Renaissance gardens to the cast-iron benches of Victorian England, garden ornaments reflect the times.

A more democratic garden tradition is based on utility. While the gardens of the nobility were decorative testaments to the timelessness of beauty, the early gardens of all but the upper classes were based on the no-nonsense need to raise food. But before long, ornamental gardening expanded its provenance.

Until recently, conformity was the rule in most gardens. Foundation plantings and wide expanses of lawn, shoulder to shoulder with neighboring yards, left little room for personal accents.

Fortunately, all that is changing. A new, eclectic garden style has emerged, allowing for individual expression through design, plantings, and ornaments. The landscape becomes a melting pot of gardening styles, ranging from Florentine urns to rustic wagon wheels to glass gazing balls.

Nature supplies the living, growing heart of the garden. We can only arrange nature's artwork to suit our tastes. But we can add a personal stamp with our choice of ornaments in the garden. These accents provide a window into the soul of the gardener. Statues, pots, and other pieces serve as metaphors for man, standing in the garden.

—Warren Schultz

Gardens and art share the same territory of the soul, invoking possibilities beyond the material. Art enhances the hidden order of nature, and gardeners realize that careful placement in the garden can elevate even the most ordinary objects to the realm of art.

ABOVE: A small set of raised beds ascending like stairsteps adds dimension to the shade garden. This design by Penelope Hobhouse eschews the standard railroad tie or landscape timber for an intricately woven wattle fence.

OPPOSITE: Benches are a welcoming touch in any garden, offering respite from a busy world. These ceramic seats establish a modern motif on the patio. The cylinder introduces pattern and color and can function as a side table, while the crouching ceramic cat adds a bit of whimsy.

ABOVE LEFT: A Florentine urn brings a classical emphasis to the garden. By planting it with boxwood, you can avoid an empty look through the winter. The mossy, weathered appearance of the urn is accented by snow.

ABOVE RIGHT: Completely intriguing and somewhat exotic, this arrangement of shells, crab claws, and stones rising on driftwood stakes above a bed of cheery nasturtiums shows an irreverence and a sense of humor, as well as creative use of natural objects, in this seaside garden.

OPPOSITE: A curved, wooden garden bench lends a Victorian air to the garden; its unfinished wood provides a counterpoint to the bed of bright spring bulbs. It's easy to imagine women in flowing white gowns and men in formal wear strolling the grounds.

OPPOSITE: Tucked in among the foxgloves, this bench is a perfect place for sharing secrets—the splashing of water over a millstone adds a background of sound to mask the words.

BELOW: A birdbath is a must to make your garden come alive with the song of feathered visitors. The classical lines of this stone birdbath fit in perfectly with the well-trimmed hedges and carefully planned perennials.

ABOVE: A small, backyard water garden is integrated into the landscape with the help of garden ornaments. These stone frogs and fish enhance the aquatic theme.

BELOW: Glossy black stones contribute a mysterious, ancient look in this Japanese garden. Though inanimate, their look changes from day to day, turning flat and gray in the sunlight, and glistening darkly in the rain.

ABOVE: The rounded form of this pergola frames a magnificent urn, which draws visitors down the path. These elements harmonize beautifully with fragrant roses and wisteria to create a sense of order and balance.

ABOVE: The best garden ornaments reinforce a sense of place. There's no doubt that you're in the Southwest when you enter this garden: if the adobe wall and plant selection don't give it away, the carved sundial, wagon wheel, and Spanish-style statuary confirm the western locale.

ABOVE: This Japanese stone pool is a study in understatement. Nearly hidden by flowers and greenery, its clean lines and neutral colors celebrate simplicity.

RIGHT: We all want our landscapes to look established, no matter how recently they were planted. The worn stones and statue add a sense of history to this herb planting. If your property isn't already endowed with such weathered features, hunt for them at architectural salvage yards.

RIGHT: The moon, the stars, the sun, indeed all of nature play a vital role in the garden. A simple wall plaque reminds us that even the smallest planting is ruled by nature's forces.

BELOW: Brightly colored molas hang from clotheslines against a rustic fence, an arrangement reminiscent of a South American marketplace. The colors mirror the flowers below and help to add a festive, exotic air to the garden.

ABOVE: Cheerful spring bulbs are paired with a brightly painted chair for a color-drenched effect. The sunny yellow chair, bright blue door, and multicolored ceramic pot unify the small plantings, which can be somewhat jarring if they're the only spots of color in the landscape.

RIGHT: Sometimes a utilitarian piece in an eye-opening color is accent enough: these watering cans brighten the green and gray backdrop. They add a casual feeling as well, as though they were just set down between tasks.

ABOVE: A dark, damp corner of a shade garden is a perfect spot for a stone gargoyle to stand watch. His inscrutable face adds an eerie quality to his surroundings, a feeling that is only heightened by the abandoned homemade broom.

OPPOSITE: The garden becomes a magical place when imagination is allowed free reign. Here, hand-blown glass decanters filled with violet- and lilac-tinted water echo the bloom colors in this city garden. The color of the water can be changed to mirror the surrounding blooms.

ABOVE: A garden accent can be as large as a house—a greenhouse in this case. The lines and sharp angles of the structure, along with its startling, white color, anchor this garden, adding a bit of order to the jumble of plants.

OPPOSITE: Rules are often suspended in rooftop gardens. Furniture, such as this mosaic table, becomes a vital element of the design. And normally earthbound plants are tended in wall-hung pots; the containers thus become an integral part of the garden plan.

ABOVE: The wheel of thyme grinds exceedingly slowly in this garden! This visual pun serves as a perfect raised bed for a tiny herb garden; several varieties can be grown efficiently in a small space while kept separate by the spokes of the wheel.

LEFT: A garden path can be one of the most influential accents in the garden. It directs visitors toward areas of special beauty, and its arrangement and spacing subtly control the traveler's pace. Here, slices of log look right at home with the natural plantings.

OPPOSITE: Cast-iron benches, a favorite of nineteenth-century gardeners, bring quaint charm to outdoor spots. The lacy, scalloped back of this bench matches the frilly edges of the old-fashioned iris in the foreground. Both plant and accent are products of the Victorian age, making a stroll down the stone path a step back in time.

PRACTICAL ACCENTS

*O*ver the course of time every garden accumulates objects: benches, pots, birdhouses, fences, trellises, sheds. It's the rare garden that consists solely of plants.

In the working landscape, utility rules. Here, items are often chosen and placed according to practical considerations, with little or no thought to their decorative value. They either recede into the background or dominate a yard.

But even the most practical of accents can be artfully fused with the landscape. First, choose a style that harmonizes with the plants and your design. Older, classical pots and benches, for example, fit in with formal perennial beds and wide expanses of lawn. Modern or rustic chairs and trellises are better suited to an informal, natural planting.

Pay attention, too, to placement. Use these practical accents to draw attention to special areas of the landscape. Or set them out of the way, where they can blend into and complement groups of plants. Consider carefully the mood of the garden, and choose your accents accordingly.

OPPOSITE: Elevating a bench is an excellent way to give it prominence in the landscape. At the same time, you're creating a seating area with a spectacular view of the garden.

RIGHT: When vines are allowed to grow over a gazebo, its lines are softened and the structure blends into the garden seamlessly. This leafy bower provides a cool refuge from the summer heat.

LEFT: This bench is a crafty blend of simplicity and sophistication, with its geometric cutouts and its cleverly inset pots. The classic terra-cotta pots can be planted with various herbs and flowers through-out the year to make the most of the season.

OPPOSITE: A brightly colored, five-legged seat is undeniably the focal point in this garden spot. The low stone wall leading to a bridge is a perfect place to sit and enjoy the landscape.

RIGHT: The garden is a creation in color, and when garden accents are part of the equation, the results can be stunning. This vibrant combination of fuchsia, terra-cotta, and wavy lines of aqua would be difficult to achieve with plants alone.

OPPOSITE: The mosaic of blooms echoes the intricate pattern of tiles on this planter. Container gardening allows tremendous variety with little investment of time or space.

RIGHT: Behold a palace fit for visitors from the heavens. Elaborate pieces, like this Oriental-style birdhouse, are often best admired against a simple backdrop of greenery.

BELOW: An unexpected coupling of plant and pot makes a dramatic statement. While a flowering plant might be an obvious choice, the clean, simple lines of an agave plant draw attention without competing with the ornate urn.

ABOVE: An eternal, uncomplaining watchman, this scarecrow steadfastly guards an herb and vegetable garden. While he may allow the occasional bird to slip by, there's no doubt that he is largely responsible for the old-fashioned, farm-country feel of his surroundings.

OPPOSITE: Gardens come alive when birds call them home. A rustic, wooden bird feeder, attractive in its own right, lures these living, flying garden ornaments.

RIGHT: The silvery gray of weathered wood and the deep green of foliage are a natural combination in the garden. A birdhouse nestled among the sedums and potted herbs imparts the tranquillity found in miniature gardens.

BELOW: Something as prosaic as a row of mailboxes becomes a delightfully practical accent when splashed with bright colors and paired with equally colorful blooms.

ABOVE: Sometimes the most successful ornamentation derives from objects placed out of context. These antique coal oil lanterns, when placed in the garden, are seen in a new light. At the same time, they can serve a practical purpose, illuminating an evening picnic or a late-night stroll.

LEFT: This charming signpost is little more than a stenciled wooden stake, yet it successfully evokes the flavor of the English countryside. Garden signs like this and vegetable and herb markers are easy to make, serve to identify your plants, and add a cozy touch to your garden.

ABOVE: Some gardens are at their best when framed by a fence. This bright Japanese fence enhances the feeling of the spare plantings and the sleek sculpture.

OPPOSITE: A charming footbridge adds a goodly dose of color while uniting the garden by spanning a little stream.

RIGHT: A wrought-iron fence holds at bay the wild garden beyond. It encloses an area without seeming impenetrable, as witnessed by the wisteria threatening to climb over and through.

FORMAL ACCENTS

*A*t some time or another, every gardener harbors dreams of grandeur. We envision our modest landscapes as kin to the great formal gardens of Europe, and we entertain the desire to invest some majesty in our own backyard.

Whether we're taken with the serious demeanor of a Renaissance parterre or the more lighthearted look of an Italian rococo garden, we all fantasize. In fact, many yards, with their rectangular shapes and broad expanses of lawn, are well-suited for a bit of classical treatment.

Formal accents can dictate the design of the garden itself, suggesting geometric patterns, straight lines, and long vistas with an ornament as the focal point. Or perhaps your garden is better suited to an Oriental simplicity with sparse plantings of simple combinations of plants and colors. Proceed with caution and with a unified sense of design, and your classical dreams can come true.

OPPOSITE: Appropriate placement, size, and tone coalesce to make this a highly successful example of classic garden ornament. The Egyptian-style statue sits in the middle of the path without obscuring the vista and the plants beyond. Its subdued color allows it to rest harmoniously in the landscape.

RIGHT: A Japanese lantern anchors a corner of a sedate landscape. Its rusty earthtones are mirrored by the rock at its base. When illuminated on a summer evening, it brings a soft luster to the garden.

ABOVE: The wealth of classical statuary in this tiny garden is almost tongue-in-cheek. The air of antiquity is emphasized by the overgrown weeds, the tangle of flowers in the planter, and the rough, tumble-down look of the stones; the spare green plant scheme doesn't include loud colors that could fight with the ornaments.

OPPOSITE: This sundial, nestled into a dense thicket of leaves, celebrates world exploration with its aged, stately ship perched atop a globe of metal bands.

ABOVE LEFT: Statues are usually placed on pedestals in the garden. By setting this bust low in the midst of a bulb bed, the gardener beautifully integrates the sculpture with the plants.

ABOVE RIGHT: Water is a desirable feature in classical gardens. The soothing sound and motion of water suggest serenity. The arching wall frames the entire arrangement.

OPPOSITE: The vertical line of this urn, set boldly atop a stone plinth, has a magnetic effect, pulling viewers toward it. Yet it is subtle enough in color, size, and shape that it doesn't vie with the planting. The tall, rather stern look of the planter tames the somewhat unruly phlox growing around it.

LEFT: An unusual, dramatic accent can transform a landscape. All eyes are drawn to this giant sunken chessboard. Most plantings would be overwhelmed by such large, imaginative garden art, but this expansive lawn extends the game board theme. The shrubs echo the playing pieces.

OPPOSITE: Mood is set by both placement and profile. Nestled against a stone wall, overgrown by ivy, and nearly obscured by centranthus, this statue creates a feeling of being absorbed by nature. The contemplative look on the face of the statue reinforces the impression.

BELOW: Exotic stone statues silently guard a wide set of stairs. The sense of mystery is enhanced by the manner in which the plants grow around them: it's as though you've stumbled into an ancient, abandoned palace garden.

ABOVE: Statues don't have to be classical in nature. This luminous blue bust juxtaposes a modern element with the primeval quality of a natural woodland garden.

OPPOSITE: With forethought and a strong sense of design, any area of the garden can serve as a site for a constructed accent. In this unusual arrangement, a trio of sculptures rises out of the pond on pedestals that recall tentacles, bridging the gap between man-made and organic forms.

RIGHT: A stone path brings order to a jubilant planting of roses and verbena. It leads, in classical fashion, to a weathered urn on a pedestal. This feature quietly beckons us forward and through the garden. The wattle fence at the end softens the feeling of enclosure.

ABOVE: A sundial takes us back to a simpler time, to an era when we weren't ruled by clocks and deadlines, and subliminally encourages us to stop and relax for a bit. The rough, uncut stone and primitive design of the piece reinforce the Edenic quality of the planting.

OPPOSITE: By its very form, art can infuse a setting with spirit. This exuberant sculpture adds a feeling of joie de vivre to a mass planting of sweet coltsfoot. It's easy to picture this wetland garden visited by sprites and spirits.

CASUAL ACCENTS

ike blank verse, an informal or modern garden at first seems easy to fashion because there are no rules to follow, no prescriptions to obey. Ironically, it is this absence of guidelines that can make planning the casual garden difficult to do well.

Anything goes in the contemporary garden: the invasion of plastic flamingos is proof of that. But not everything works. Even if the mood of your garden is light and whimsical, accents should be carefully chosen and artfully placed. The plants should always be given center stage, with ornaments taking a supporting, albeit important, role.

Consider the feeling you want your garden to convey. The range of accents you can find for a casual garden allows you to use folk art to create a cozy oasis or to incorporate kitschy pieces that amuse your visitors. This is the perfect opportunity to infuse your garden with your own personality, whether it be warm and earthy or playfully outrageous.

OPPOSITE: Gardens provide a link to the past, to a time when life was less complicated. Here, an antique water pump helps build the illusion of stepping back in time. The plantings around it are kept simple to further that feeling.

RIGHT: Formal topiary in pots contrasts with a rough, wooden chair that looks not far removed from the tree that supplied the material. The dark form of a globular vase adds a modern touch and repeats the undulating lines of the sun mosaic.

ABOVE: When choosing ornaments for the garden, select those that preserve a sense of the region. Formal garden art would seem out of place in this Southwestern xeriscape planting. But a mosaic dais, paired with a simple birdhouse, captures the simple, geometric patterns of Native American art.

OPPOSITE: Indoors, the function of a birdcage sometimes overrides its graceful form. But outdoors, adorning a mottled, vermilion wall, this rainbow-colored aviary, grounded by the potted geraniums below, completes a perfect garden picture.

RIGHT: A patio or balcony railing transcends the functional with the aid of a few fanciful elements. At the same time, it's an ideal location to hang flowering plants like these geraniums.

ABOVE: The sweeping, almost musical form of a sundial soars from a bed of herbs in a modern city garden. Nearby, a redwood bench with an unusual, sunrise-shaped back offers a place to sit and watch the passage of time.

LEFT: The spare form of a metal sundial mellows when morning glories are encouraged to creep in and contribute their brilliant color to the scene.

OPPOSITE: Often, unused structures on a property can be turned to advantage rather than torn down. Here, an old stone well has been transformed into a rising rock garden with a planting of sedums and other rock garden plants. The embellished wrought-iron pail support arching over the well supplies additional architectural interest.

ABOVE: Folk art, too, makes a welcome accent in a casual setting. This primitive carved and painted statue adds a Caribbean feeling to the garden. The bright beads link the piece to the dazzling colors of the surrounding plantings.

OPPOSITE: Woven vines make fine weatherproof material for garden accents. They can be fashioned into any number of imaginative shapes and forms, such as these woven wood geese.

ABOVE: Kitchen gardens of the eighteenth century inspired this little plot, where a bee skep on a pedestal holds a place of honor. These hives, made of twisted straw, attract bees to pollinate plants and provide a source of honey. Nowadays, they are often purely ornamental, lending a traditional, homey touch to any garden.

LEFT: A rustic gazebo, reminiscent of a crude hayrack, effectively punctuates this wetland space without disrupting the wild feel. Built exclusively of natural materials, it looks almost like a nest for humans.

OPPOSITE: Even meadows and wildflower gardens can be improved by an accent. This gardener brings focus and a sense of history to the site by placing a traditional Southwestern horno oven in the midst of black-eyed Susans, sunflowers, daisies, and other blooms. The shape and color of the clay oven tie the entire landscape to the bluffs in the distance.

ABOVE LEFT: At their best, garden accents seduce visitors into viewing more than the scene immediately before them: rather than competing with the garden itself, effective ornaments offer encouragement to take in the entire sweep of the plantings. Though the bright red geraniums in the foreground may attract first attention, the bleached skull hanging from the adobe wall draws the eye to the back of the garden to automatically survey all the beds in between.

ABOVE RIGHT: Some of the most effective ornaments are the most simple. These shiny river stones in a small stream add a sense of serenity. Their shapes and texture create a transition between the running water and the upright plants. The tiny stone frogs bring the arrangement to life.

OPPOSITE: With the adobe walls and bricks carrying the feel of the desert into this garden room, the deadwood planter appears natural and completely in scale. It takes only a few common petunias to turn an old log into a charming garden accent.

ABOVE: The fresh-looking color scheme of luminous white flowers and green leaves and pots has been carried over to the antique watering can. The sizable dent somehow adds to the charm, convincing us that the can has been well used and the potted garden has been well tended.

LEFT: Ivy drifts across the face of a plaster plaque, creating the illusion of clouds moving to cover the sun. Well-placed garden ornaments not only add a decorative element, they can also bring a new dimension to the plants.

OPPOSITE: Playfulness grows in this garden. An elaborate fountain constructed of shells offers a strong clue to this gardener's disposition. The visual rhyme of shells and water, along with the whimsical mask of Hermes, leaves no doubt that this person enjoys the garden.

ACCENTS IN THE LANDSCAPE

*I*nfatuation with ornaments should not be allowed to grow into blind love. Remember that accents are intended to highlight the plantings, not upstage them.

Always keep the mood of your garden in mind when choosing ornaments, and plan the type of ornament according to the garden style. Classical pieces will always enhance a formal garden, while modern or folk art is more appropriate for a casual garden.

Beyond that advice, there are a few guidelines to follow:

• Be aware of scale. Ornaments should not overpower a small planting or recede to the point of oblivion in a large one.

• Consider sight lines and perspective. Choose accents with strong vertical elements for open expanses of lawn; cluster smaller objects in corners of plantings.

• Note the way light and shadow play across your garden. Place large objects where rays of sunlight will spotlight them during certain periods of the day. Or nestle small objects in shady nooks. Use vines, trees, and plants with plentiful foliage as backdrops for statues or brightly colored ornaments.

• Look for natural curves or upright habits in plants and mirror them with arching or vertical accents.

• Keep an eye out for the best vantage points for accents. Place ornaments so that they can be enjoyed from patios, porches, walkways, or windows.

Finally, have fun accenting your landscape, and don't be afraid to take a chance by violating the rules.

OPPOSITE: A stone urn overflowing with marguerites, helichrysum, and nicotiana immediately attracts attention: the delicate flowering plants are lifted to a place of honor. If planted in the ground, they might have been overlooked or overpowered by other plants.

ABOVE: Sometimes there's impact in numbers. Found objects often make the greatest impression when they're grouped together. The combination of textures, materials, shapes, and colors makes this an interesting corner of a wild landscape.

ABOVE: A thoughtful garden design matches accents with plants and with the overall milieu of the garden. This worn and weathered chair would look unkempt on a lawn, but it seems perfectly at home tucked beneath a similarly weathered picket fence covered with rambling, old-fashioned roses.

LEFT: Design and form can provide important cues for good placement of accents. The rustic material, simple design, and subdued colors of this handmade chair coordinate perfectly with the farmlike setting.

OPPOSITE: A healthy dose of imagination can result in accents that quite literally become part of the garden. Here, simple kitchen chairs take on a fairy tale aspect when planted with moss and wrapped in twisting vines. They ensure that this spot of the garden will continue to entertain even through the winter months.

ABOVE: The coppery sheen of the shallow pool's bottom sets off the green of the surrounding herbs, while the border of verdigris tiles extends the leafy theme. The water enhances the beauty of the plants by reflecting their image in its surface.

RIGHT: A simple stone basin makes a fine garden accent all through the year. But placed beneath a maple, it is bound to catch the leaves from above, making it come alive with red and gold in the autumn.

OPPOSITE: A unique arrangement of turf and stone in a checker-board design fits best in the corner of a wide expanse of lawn. The hulking shrubs serve as living metaphors for chess pieces.

RIGHT: Diminutive, churchlike birdhouses, complete with steeples, are a welcome surprise when removed from their normal, airy location and placed near the ground amid a grouping of terra-cotta pots. They emphasize the flowering plants by bringing a new focus to the scene.

OPPOSITE: An old stone springhouse has been incorporated into this picturesque water garden. Reminiscent of an ancient grotto, it provides a natural transition from the bog planting to the dry-land plants surrounding it. Flowers planted atop the structure help to integrate it into the landscape.

BELOW: An unmowed meadow scattered with spikes of foxglove looks almost like an accidental planting. Carefully overturn some textured urns in a variety of earthy hues, and the entire scene comes together with the mystery of an ancient tableau.

ABOVE: Some ornaments work best when they are made to mimic nature. These whimsical rabbits peer out from foliage to delight passing children and other nature lovers.

OPPOSITE: The style and color of an accent should be carefully selected to fit the surrounding garden. This artful, monochromatic piece complements the planting with its simplicity of form. The green foliage, in turn, allows the statue its place in the sun.

≈ *Part Two* ≈

POTS AND
CONTAINERS

INTRODUCTION

Container plantings have had a long and glorious role in the history of gardening. From the hanging gardens of Babylon to the Renaissance gardens of Italy, gardeners have planted in pots. There's something special about a container garden. It integrates art and nature, and shows the hand of humankind amidst nature's will.

Today, the garden is more than a place for plants. Naturally, plants are still the focal point, but other elements, such as containers, help to sharpen that focus. We all want to bring our own sense of style to our gardens. Containers and pots offer a great way of doing just that, without trying to gild the lily.

Container gardening has come a long way from a simple pot of marigolds on the steps and even beyond hanging baskets and window boxes. Just as we shop carefully for furnishings for the interiors of our homes, so should we carefully furnish our outdoor garden rooms, whether it's a front porch, deck or patio, or even a formal border.

As we move out into the landscape for living and entertaining, we no longer confine our plants to those all-too-rare ideal sunny spaces. We want our plants to work harder for us. We ask them to bring the appeal of growing plants to areas where they might not otherwise reach.

Container gardens bridge the gap between plants and garden hardscape in the landscape. They help to integrate a sculptural element into the garden, and at the same time bring the softness of greenery to patios, steps, and pavement.

There's something addictive and alluring about container planting. Start with a simple window box or hanging basket, and you'll soon find yourself surveying the garden for other sites. —*Warren Schultz*

OPPOSITE: Containers allow the gardener to bring plants close to living areas. A cluster of exuberant petunias, impatiens, and geraniums offers the illusion of the garden inching its way onto the dining courtyard.

ABOVE: Though container plantings are usually thought of as seasonal accents, don't be in a hurry to empty the pot when frost strikes. Many plants can serve as attention getters even in the off-season. A filigree of frost on these hydrangea blossoms keeps the spirit of the garden alive well into the winter.

LEFT: Pots can accentuate the understated garden, attracting attention with a whisper of color. *Hosta* and *Camassia*, each in its own simple pot, grace this shady brick fountain.

BELOW: A sense of stability is brought to a court-yard with a carefully arranged planting of finely trimmed shrubs in containers. They'll provide lively interest throughout each season.

OPPOSITE: Even an ordinary brick garage can be dressed up when it's surrounded by and draped with plants. Hanging baskets, window boxes, and pots can be combined to present a wall of plants that make this corner of the garden come alive.

ABOVE: Containers allow the artful juxtaposition of disparate plants in the landscape. The common garden nasturtium takes on an exotic air when planted around a potted palm.

BELOW: Just a few containers of plants can present many types of architectural forms. From the strongly vertical mahonias and roses in the background to draping ivies in the foreground, these plants shape this entryway.

OPPOSITE: Different shapes, sizes, and materials can be combined with good effect when planning container plantings. The pots serve as focal points, leading the eye and the visitor through the garden.

OPPOSITE: A courtyard or doorway can be enriched by a combination of plants in pots. Simple color patterns provide a welcoming feel, and the bright colors offer a hint at the type of welcome the visitor can expect to receive.

ABOVE: Container planters don't have to be large and imposing to make a splash, nor do the plants have to be bright. Sometimes a more subdued treatment is called for, such as this stone trough planted with alpines.

LEFT: At their best, containers enliven a landscape or hardscape without violating its spirit. Nothing could be simpler than red geraniums in a window box; the mass of a single, bright color blends beautifully with the effect of a weathered window.

BELOW: Where a splash of color is needed, a potted plant can fill the bill. A seasonal shrub such as this hydrangea can serve to brighten up a dark corner. The plant can be moved to a sunnier spot when its blooming season is over.

OPPOSITE: Of course, plants in pots are portable. That's one of their best features. A movable feast of flowers encourages a changing scene through the seasons. Pots and plants can be arranged to present different scenes from week to week.

ABOVE: Containers themselves can add a dynamic element to a planting. A well-worn terra-cotta pot contains the exuberance of the bright, brazen combination of red and orange. The pot helps to integrate the planting with the wall behind it.

RIGHT: Container plantings can be playful and whimsical. Appreciation is heightened by juxtaposition, or the surprise of finding plants that you would expect to see only in the ground. These miniature sunflowers delight in the simplicity of their strong vertical lines.

OPPOSITE: The garden can go where it's never gone before when part of it is planted in pots. Well-placed containers help the garden to be viewed from inside the house. Bright geraniums and crisp white *Nicotiana* add a welcome splash of color to a brick courtyard.

ABOVE LEFT: Even in the height of the season, gardeners often find themselves plying their trade in areas without plants. Simple, small potted geraniums can be moved to provide color and closeness even in such places as a potting shed.

ABOVE RIGHT: A careful container planting offers a sense of place. A single Japanese maple planted in a stone-mulched container sets an oriental scene.

THE POT'S THE THING

*I*n the garden, containers are much more than places to put plants. They can add an artistic touch to the landscape with colors, forms, and textures of their own. In their design, they may bring a sense of tradition to the landscape.

Containers may be made of materials from plastic to plaster. The material itself can set a mood and fulfill a style. Plastic is utilitarian. Lightweight and durable, it lends itself to experimentation. Stone feels solid and established. Wood has a rustic feel that fits in well with a cottage garden. Cast-iron or concrete urns lend a formal feel. Terra-cotta is a simple and time-honored substance.

Containers are versatile. The pots themselves can become a design element, or they may recede to the background when the plants are in full bloom. During other times of the season, they may be more prominent.

Choosing containers offers a chance to exercise creativity. Nearly anything that holds soil—as long as it provides adequate drainage—can serve as a planter. Boots, old rowboats, and cans and jars can all be creative choices for containers, but pay attention to scale and size: the height of the plants should equal the depth of the container.

You can group pots of disparate materials together for an exciting, vibrant, informal feel. Utilize classical urns or stone planters in a formal landscape, or get into the spirit and break the rules by putting your personal stamp on a container planting.

OPPOSITE: Jardinieres were common plant holders in the 1950s until they fell out of favor. Ready to make a comeback, this jardiniere holds a planting of *Oxypetalum caeruleum* along a walk.

ABOVE: It takes a bright flower, such as ranunculus, to hold its own against an unusual container like this primitive stone planting bowl.

LEFT: Creative placement can enable us to view plants in a different light. Simple red geraniums are elevated to a new level of elegance with this imaginative arrangement.

BELOW: Sometimes the plant dictates the container. Epiphytic orchids that grow naturally on the bark of trees need only a bit of support, allowing them to thrive in this unusual slatted container.

OPPOSITE: The speckled blue glaze of this planter complements the pastel pink hyacinths growing from it. The short, upright plants don't detract from the pot.

OPPOSITE: A trailing plant, such as verbena, is a perfect match for a low, wide terra-cotta pot.

ABOVE LEFT: Simple pots for simple plants is a good rule to follow (and sometimes break). Simple coats of paint take these terra-cotta pots beyond the obvious, while the white-faced pansies provide perfect accompaniment to the bright colors.

ABOVE RIGHT: Containers can serve as valued garden accents, suggesting mood and style. This bas-relief terra-cotta pot, planted with early daffodils, brings instant elegance to a garden corner.

ABOVE: When the container is unusual, such as this painted window box, it pays to keep the planting simple. Here, a single color of geranium is all that's required.

RIGHT: A wire basket lined with peat moss makes an unusual and elegant container for a mix of annual flowers. When it's placed artfully on a pedestal of stones in a stream, the effect is eye-popping.

OPPOSITE: Containers can be chosen to match the form and feel of surrounding plants. A classic urn mirrors the curve of the topiary planted nearby. The ivy and clipped box planted in the urn carry the effect even further.

OPPOSITE: Bathing, anyone? It might look ludicrous stuck in the middle of a lawn or on a front terrace, but tucked into an overgrown corner of the garden and planted with *Corydalis*, this old bathtub makes a statement that's both whimsical and tasteful.

BELOW: Some of the most successful containers are those that were made to hold something else. An old milk can with its tall, straight lines and burnished look takes on a new life as a pot.

ABOVE: A woven wicker basket provides just the right touch as the perfect perch for a topiary bird.

ABOVE: A weathered lead trough proves to be the perfect container for a bonsai, providing just the right feel of age and elegance.

LEFT: These boots were made for planting. An informal garden will gladly accept just about anything that will hold soil and water as a container. Ajuga and violas find these old shoes easy to fill.

LEFT: Suggesting a flower seller's cart and bringing a sense of motion to a quiet courtyard corner, an old wheelbarrow makes a fine planter for these ferns and hydrangeas.

BELOW: The natural, glowing patterns of a wooden trough soften the hard surroundings. Gently trailing plants allow the container to garner attention.

CONTAINERS IN THE LANDSCAPE

The laws of landscaping the garden that pertain to beds and borders apply to container plantings as well. Anyone can plant a geranium in a pot and place it in the corner of a deck, but when a sense of daring and design is brought to container gardening, the planting becomes an integral part of the landscape.

Container gardens are meant to attract attention. Start in an area where they have the most impact—an entryway, patio, or porch—then work from there to expand your container horizons.

Consider symmetry and repetition. A single potted arrangement may look awkward, but pair it with another container planting and you have instant balance. Don't forget contrast: a container of brightly blooming annuals breaks up a spread of lawn or pavement just as a subdued urn of foliage plants will add some weight to a border planting.

Scale is important. Small container plantings get lost in large areas. Huge pots on a patio may be too imposing. And don't neglect the vertical dimension. Place pots on steps or on top of walls. Utilize plant stands and hanging planters. They'll immediately add a new proportion to a landscape.

Consider the dimension of time as well. Containers allow you to alter plantings and accents as no grounded garden can. Start with bulbs in spring, then continue on to elements that will add interest in autumn and even through the winter.

The beauty of containers is that they encourage the gardener to experiment.

OPPOSITE: Pots brimming with foliage and blooms emphasize the opulence of this informal backyard cottage garden.

ABOVE: Tucked into a brick-lined alcove, this container planting provides a single splash of color. The hanging ivy echoes the graceful lines of the surroundings.

BELOW: Just a few well-chosen pots, carefully placed, impose a sense of order on a cacophony of blooms. Here, potted plants provide a connection between the two levels of the garden. One trick is to fill them with plants that aren't found in the garden. This gardener has chosen *Allium chelsea* and *Phormium* 'Bronze Baby'.

ABOVE: In the city, where open ground is scarce, a planting may be as simple as a single pot full of plants. Early blooming flowers such as pansies can brighten up a spot long before garden beds are ready to flower.

OPPOSITE: A cluster of pots provides a centerpiece in a gravel courtyard and transforms an otherwise barren spot. This garden of conifers and alpines is enhanced by the variety of pot shapes and materials.

BELOW: Potted plants may be used as accents to highlight the best features of an in-ground planting. These small potted box-woods complement the topiary in the background. A casually placed watering can completes the scene.

OPPOSITE: Urns can be situated in a hidden area or at the end of a path to provide a destination, thus heightening the drama of an area. A simple planting of *Lamium* takes on new life situated here.

ABOVE: Container plantings can be combined with in-ground garden beds to add a touch of elegance. This feeling is enhanced when a stately specimen, such as this bay, is surrounded by plants in a simple, formal pattern.

ABOVE: At their best, container plantings allow plants to be seen in a new light. Flowers normally found underfoot, such as this spring-blooming *Muscari*, can be lifted into better view.

OPPOSITE: When planted with standard shrubs and trees, containers can add a sense of permanence and stability to a small city terrace.

OPPOSITE: Containers help to bring the planting right to the front door. Pots filled with impatiens add a whimsical sense of motion to the scene as though the plants themselves were climbing the stairs.

ABOVE: By placing pots in unfamiliar surroundings and unusual arrangements, this gardener has added new drama to a container planting. Hung from a brick wall and spilling out onto a courtyard, these plants are more varied than any in-ground planting could ever be.

ABOVE: Clay pots of dwarf oleander rise against the backdrop of the big sky of the Southwest. The sparse and rough foliage fits the climate, while the pots are integrated with the architecture.

LEFT: A pot of simple red petunias adds a dramatic splash of color to a Southwestern courtyard. The theme is carried through by a small pot well placed in a corner. Even the empty pottery adds drama to the scene.

OPPOSITE: An intriguing arrangement of container plants combines various textures and colors, and integrates them into a pleasing union.

OPPOSITE: A simple stucco urn adds form and life to a scene. The wall of ivy, severely clipped, is softened by the lines and colors of the container and the plants that grow from it.

LEFT: Potted plants can be combined with their in-ground counterparts for a great effect. At their best, the pots may be barely noticed. Planting in pots allows you to move them to the focal point of a garden while the flowers are in bloom, then move them out of the way as they fall to foliage.

BELOW: When a container is brimming with plants, the overall look is abundance and vitality. These containers are completely obscured by hanging and trailing annuals that seem to grow magically in midair.

CONTAINER COMBINATIONS

ive a gardener a big enough pot, and there's virtually no plant that can't be grown out of the ground. There are hundreds of species of flowering and foliage plants that grow contentedly in pots, and there is an innumerable number of combinations that one can use.

Container gardening offers the plant lover a chance to sharpen his or her design sense. A container planting is a garden in microcosm. Each plant decision should be considered carefully. The first thing to attend to is not appearance but cultural requirements. Remember, these plants will be squeezed together in the same environment. They must have similar needs for sunlight, water, and soil. In other words, don't try to plant a cactus with a hosta.

When choosing plants to share a pot, also consider form. Combining upright plants with trailing ones works well. Keep in mind the flower shape and size. Be aware that there are several ways to use color combinations. It depends on the kind of statement you want the pots to make. For an elegant look, confine pots to a single color or a pair of pastels. For a more informal and energetic look, combine primary colors. Don't forget foliage: green or variegated foliage helps to separate bright colors and refreshes the eye.

Blooming season is important. When there's room for only a few plants, they all have to work hard. You can't afford the luxury of plants such as many perennials that bloom for only a few weeks. Or if you do, you must combine them with plants that will do yeoman's duty all season long.

OPPOSITE: Container plantings offer numerous opportunities for artful arrangement. This mass of colorful *Pelargonium* is framed by the succulent spiky agaves and the cool blue-green shades of the sansevierias.

ABOVE: A low container makes a perfect home for a collection of spring bulbs. Here, *Narcissus* 'Mount Hood' is surrounded by small clumps of hyacinths, with tiny, white polyanthus blooms sprinkled throughout.

LEFT: Pots don't have to be paired to make a harmonious picture. There's a temptation to plant identical combinations when two pots are placed in the landscape. Here, the gardener has produced the maximum effect by giving each container planting its own identity, with pastel-colored *Pelargonium* in one pot and bright yellow marguerites in the other.

ABOVE: Placing singly potted plants in a basket gives each plant the attention it deserves. Bright, pendulous tuberous begonias steal the show, but taller daisies add an informal accent along with the purple foliage of opal basil.

ABOVE: Hanging containers offer the gardener a great opportunity to combine form and flower in an interesting way. Bright red upright fuchsias offer a contrast to trailing purple petunias, red verbenas, and impatiens in pink and white.

RIGHT: Small pots call for simple designs and basic colors. This shallow Chinese bowl is planted with a combination of all-white violas and marguerites.

OPPOSITE: Climbing, flowering passion vine forms a perfect backdrop for a container of marigolds, *Nicotianana*, and *Helichrysum*.

OPPOSITE: A combination of tulips and pansies says it's springtime. The blazing tulips, which stretch skyward, appear as flames rising from a lamp. Pure white pansies offer dramatic contrast.

ABOVE: Spiky *Cordyline* rises dramatically from a large clay pot. Its strong vertical nature is softened by a cloud of trailing geraniums.

ABOVE: Bright yellow tulips are allowed to predominate in this simple, small planter. White pansies peeking out from behind add just a touch of variety.

RIGHT: Carefully arranged and planted, a window box can contain bundles and layers of blossom. There's an appealing sense of order to these geraniums, lobelias, impatiens, and petunias kept in bounds.

OPPOSITE: There's no limit to the different looks of a simple combination of two types of plants. Purple pansies provide continuity when planted in four different pots. Tulips in bright colors add variety.

OPPOSITE: At the end of the season, autumn plants in pots can be gathered to provide a bright farewell to summer. The red and rusty colors of *Spiraea* 'Golden Princess', *Erica*, *Dendranthemum*, and *Gaultheria* make an eye-catching combination.

LEFT: Containers allow the gardener to vary plant combinations with each season. This autumn grouping features white ornamental cabbage, and trailing ivy, along with *Euonymus*, *Brachyglottis*, and *Skimmia*.

BELOW: This bright combination of yellow blooms and variegated leaves is a cheery accent to this window.

PRACTICAL PLANTERS

More than just a place to put pretty plants, containers can be put to work, too. Containers can help the gardener overcome daunting conditions—shade, poor soil, lack of space—and enable one to grow food-producing crops.

Short on space? Lacking the acreage for a harvest of fruit or vegetables? Never have enough herbs near the kitchen door? Overcoming these problems are what containers are for.

Herbs are perfect for container gardening. Most are small, easy to maintain in pots, and attractive all through the growing season. You can combine an entire spice rack in a single container. Tricolor thyme and purple sage in a pot are a welcome sight at anyone's back door. With a little care, they'll keep producing their fragrant and flavorful leaves throughout the season.

But you needn't confine yourself to small plants. Even humble vegetable garden denizens—lettuce, cucumbers, and peppers—seem to take on a new aura when featured in containers. Indeed, tomatoes rising from a pot or cascading from a hanging planter can become a patio attraction.

Growing food in containers offers many advantages. Plants can be kept close to the house to provide easy protection from frost. They can be nestled against a wall or into protected pockets. It's hard to neglect them, and harvesting them is easy.

OPPOSITE: Herb gardens shine in container plantings, especially those designed in a formal parterre style. Lemon balm in a terra-cotta pot rises above these carefully arranged herbs.

ABOVE: A patio provides the perfect setting for a group of medieval herbs, including a topiary rosemary, bay, and acanthus. With each in its own pot, they can be arranged for maximum effect through the growing season.

ABOVE: A strawberry planter is put to work doing what it does best—growing a crop of strawberries, just enough for breakfast. It's flanked by simple clay pots that house chives and parsley.

OPPOSITE: A low, shallow pot provides the ground for an artfully arranged herb garden of various types of thyme.

ABOVE: Pushed to the limits, containers can work all kinds of wonders. Even a sprawling tomato plant loaded with ripe fruit can thrive in a small window box. In the city, nothing says summer like strolling out to the sidewalk to pick a fresh, juicy tomato.

RIGHT: Planters can be pretty as well as practical. Even common vegetables such as cabbage carry good looks, especially when combined with marigolds and nasturtiums.

ABOVE: There is a world of fascinating, glorious-looking edibles perfect for containers. These striking yellow and white miniature eggplants grow happily in a wooden bucket along with an understory of lettuce for a summer salad.

RIGHT: Containers offer the perfect solution to the problem of tender herbs. In summer, rosemary can be grown outdoors where it makes a lush, stately statement at a dooryard, then can be moved into a protected place for the winter.

RIGHT: A standard clay pot can provide a season's worth of salad ingredients. Even small lettuce plants make an attractive planting in a shallow container.

BELOW: A green wave of parsley makes an elegant border along a rose garden and provides enough seasoning to satisfy even the most prolific chef.

BELOW: The combination of different plants in one container can help each plant to fulfill its ornamental potential. A layer of Italian parsley hides the bare stalk of this eggplant, making it all the more attractive.

OPPOSITE: This gardener has grown a virtual produce section on the steps of a patio. Rainbow pots overflow with a bounty of lettuce, tomatoes, peppers, and herbs.

ABOVE: Harkening back to the orangeries of Renaissance Europe, a citrofortunella in an elegant urn provides a tropical feel, even in northern landscapes.

RIGHT: Where sunshine is plentiful but bare ground is in short supply, anyone can have a thriving vegetable garden. All it takes is a bunch of generous pots and regular watering to harvest tomatoes and peppers on a courtyard.

BELOW: Container plantings can sometimes surprise and amuse. Who would expect to find cabbage growing eight feet (2.4m) overhead? A hanging basket provides plenty of room for a healthy planting.

ABOVE: Some herbs are very picky, with individual demands when it comes to growing conditions. Watercress, as expected, requires more moisture than cilantro, chives, or lettuce. By planting each in its own pot, care is simplified.

ABOVE: A strawberry jar planted with purple sage, thyme, rosemary, and oriental chives looks like an island oasis rising from a sea of green.

OPPOSITE: There's not a berry in sight, but this strawberry pot still serves a useful purpose. In fact, it's a perfect way to make a varied herb garden in a small space. Rosemary, sage, oregano, and lavender provide a cupboard full of spice as they grow up and over the pot.

Part Three
SEATS AND BENCHES

INTRODUCTION

Gardens, whether large or small, filled with lawns and shrubs, flower beds and borders, or rows of herbs and vegetables, provide the natural settings for homes. They offer protection from neighbors as well as a means of integrating homes into neighborhoods. Gardens are created to be admired by passersby and enjoyed by owners. They may be planted with their bounty in mind or designed to provide a fair-weather living space, but whether more time is spent caring for gardens or relaxing in them, all garden lovers are glad to find a place to pause and sit amid the beauty.

An important element in garden design, garden furniture should enhance the landscaping and should be selected with the same attention given to the plantings. It is equally important, however, to choose practical seating that suits your needs. Are you looking for true comfort or for a place to catch your breath? Do you wish to sit in the open or in shelter? Will the seat allow you to take advantage of a view or be the focus of one? Do you want to recline, read, or dine? Should your seating be stationary, or will you want to move it about? And lastly, your garden furniture should please your fancy.

INTEGRATING SEATS AND BENCHES WITH YOUR LANDSCAPE

Seats and benches placed within a garden invite outdoor relaxation. The style of garden furniture you select should be in keeping with the style of your garden—and with the architecture of your home if they will be viewed together. The more formal your landscaping, the more formal your seats and benches are likely to be; conversely, the more naturalistic the setting, the more rustic you may wish your furnishings. Gardens, like interiors, should be furnished with pieces that are in proportion to the space they will occupy, that complement and enhance the mood and style of the environment and the occupants. That being said, bear in mind that gardens are living and constantly changing places, and the history of garden design is filled with contrivance, conceit, and folly where humans have successfully inserted as many surprises as nature. As long as you understand the attitude you wish your garden to embody, you should feel free to trust your instincts and choose seats or benches that beckon you.

As you think about what sort of garden seating to select, consider whether your seats and benches will be prominent features of your landscape or tucked into intimate settings. Will they be adjacent to other structural elements—walkways, patios, arbors, walls, or even buildings—or set among trees, lawns, or borders? Also, don't neglect the changing of the seasons as you choose the material or color of your furnishings—be sure you will like them once flowers and foliage have faded. There are countless charming garden seats and benches to choose from—all with various maintenance requirements and, of course, varying costs, which will no doubt also influence your choice.

—Carol Spier

OPPOSITE: The airy white bench in this formal garden has a sprightly, upright attitude very much in keeping with the standard fruit trees it faces. The scrolled and woven metal is reminiscent of an elegant eighteenth-century bird cage, and although decorative enough to be important in this space, the bench is delicate and neither obscures nor overpowers the plantings.

ABOVE: Simple, gently curved stone benches mark the perimeter of this formal clearing, inviting the stroller to sit, enjoy the sun, and contemplate the garland-carrying statue. Stone is a classic material for garden ornament; it weathers well and quickly assumes an aspect of antiquity that is prized by many landscape designers—which is most appropriate to this setting.

RIGHT: The rustic stone bench in the middle of this backyard garden is simplicity itself and suits the shingled New England home behind it. The dwarf Alberta spruce trees that flank the gray bench will provide a green accent when the country flowers die back, giving the bench definition in wintertime.

OPPOSITE: This brick cottage is delightfully overgrown with climbing roses that transform its facade into a vertical garden. A weathered wood chair sits by the stoop, complementing perfectly the aged door and window. A visitor calling when no one is at home might choose to wait and perhaps drowse peacefully in perfumed sunlight.

ABOVE: Garden seats are often strategically placed to offer repose or a view at the end of a walk or prospect. Here, a classic Lutyens bench beckons at the end of a rose bower.

LEFT: The small glade of trees at the end of this large country lawn shelters a formal cast iron bench, which is a surprising contrast to the unpretentious setting but so charming and inviting as it comes into view.

OPPOSITE: Here, a circular drive skirts a spot of lawn covered by a bower of blooming fruit trees. Rustic twig benches sit informally below, catching the spirit of the branching limbs; later in the season, they will offer a casual and shady outdoor respite from the hot sun.

ABOVE: Providing a colorful edge to a lawn or terrace, perennial borders are usually admired and strolled past. An inviting bench has been tucked discreetly into this one, offering a fragrant spot to read, repose, or watch a game being played on the lawn.

OPPOSITE: Soon to be a vine-covered arbor, this formal green bench sits at the end of a tailored lawn that serves as a patio. The arch of the arbor repeats in the back of the bench.

ABOVE: Lest anyone forget, gardens are workplaces as well as showplaces, and you will probably be glad to have a resting place when planting, pruning, weeding, or harvesting yours. A carved wood bench is a welcome fixture in this walled New Mexican garden—a good choice in the terra-cotta-colored Spanish ambiance.

LEFT: When designing your landscape, consider creating a small garden around a bench. Here, a built-in seat embraces assorted stone pavings and is in turn framed with effusive cosmos and small potted bamboo. The mood is somewhat oriental and the effect much more interesting than a plot of flowers cut into the lawn.

ABOVE: Given some thought, found objects can be fashioned into garden seating in a formal landscape. This weathered plank resting on mossy stones beside a graveled path appears to have grown here; its grays and greens, rounds and flats meld harmoniously with the setting.

OPPOSITE: Wonderful chairs and benches can sometimes be discovered in the landscape, creating naturalistic and unobtrusive informal garden seating. A fallen branch may offer the perfect resting spot, as on this hillside where a large curved limb has been leveled with stones.

SITING SEATS AND BENCHES

*I*f you are thinking about adding a chair or bench to your garden, your first consideration will probably be its location. The setting you choose for your furniture will most likely influence your choice of its style or design. While the site may be dictated by special needs such as offering a resting place along a long path or providing a spot to sit back out of the sun in a working garden, the location of garden furniture is more likely to be a matter of aesthetics, giving focus to a special feature—a view, a pool, a clearing or court, or an intimate spot—and allowing you to take advantage of it. Once you know where you want to place your chair, you will be able to decide how many people it should accommodate, if it should be built-in or movable, and what material, shape, and color it should be to best enhance the setting.

FOR A LONG VISTA

If your garden offers a prospect—a scenic view of sunrise or sunset, of neighboring woods, water, or meadows, or even of your own fairly large lawn, you will no doubt want to be able to sit down to enjoy it in comfort.

ABOVE: In a pastoral setting with a breathtaking view such as this, a rough-hewn slab bench is unobtrusive and inviting. While almost any bench would suit this lovely spot, there is something particularly appealing about one that owes little to the hand of man. You might, however, prefer a structure with a back so that you could lean back and relax.

OPPOSITE: This rolling country lawn has been broken up with interior hedges and flower beds that give it a sense of accessibility in spite of its large area. Benches placed within each section offer both long and short views and the possibility of sun or shade.

ABOVE: Benches tucked into the plantings at the edge or corner of a large lawn will appear and feel much more intimate than those set out in the open, even though they offer a wide prospect of the landscape and are in full view.

BY THE WATERSIDE

Water in a garden is an enticing, beckoning feature. It catches the light, moves with the wind, and reflects its surroundings; it may be natural or man-made, still or moving, planted or swimmable, but it is always fascinating. Whether you have a fountain, a lily pond, a reflecting pool, a meandering stream, or a sparkling cascade, you should be able to relax and dream beside it in comfort, so place an inviting seat nearby.

ABOVE: It would be difficult to resist basking in the sunlight at the edge of this lovely lily pond. Although one half of the pond is bordered with mature shrubbery, the prospect across the yard is open and might be spoiled by a heavy or self-important piece of furniture; this classic park bench is perfectly balanced with the site and sits in graceful repose, inviting company.

ABOVE: A bench built to encircle a tree trunk can be almost as magical as water, so what better choice for relaxing by a woodland pond? This one, designed with simple but thoughtful detail, has weathered nicely into its natural setting.

RIGHT: Fanciful wire-backed chairs sit in delicate contrast to a stone-framed pond. Unoccupied, their delicate tracery appears vinelike against the boulders.

ABOVE: Here, a simple stone slab perched atop stone supports blends with the organic edge that frames this goldfish pond. Ferns, flowers, and fish abound in this quiet nook.

As a Focal Point

Strategically placed seats and benches can be used to call attention to an important feature or area of your garden—or to create one. Use them to draw the eye, as well as the body, toward a specimen planting, a patio, a turn in a walkway, or a distant corner.

ABOVE: You need not start with a large parklike space nor an enticing natural feature to create an elegant garden. This yard has been thoughtfully enclosed and planned with simple but effective formality. The regularity of the design leads the eye to the central slate terrace, where a group of wicker chairs is ready for friendly discourse.

RIGHT: This aged and magnificent tree stands importantly in the center of a large and open lawn. While the eye is drawn in wonder to the tree's girth, the clean white bench encircling the trunk begs you to wander over for a closer look.

ABOVE: Paths in gardens large and small must lead somewhere—even if only to the property line. A bench viewed at the end of a path gives importance to the walk ahead. Here, a mown grass path leads irresistibly to an elegant and cleverly designed seat.

OPPOSITE: If you have a country estate large enough to offer the prospect of a distant seat, then place it where it can be seen from porch or window. Here, a wonderful cast iron bench beckons you to rest under the honeysuckle and roses in the corner of a walled lawn.

As a Retreat

If your garden includes an intimate bower, a hidden nook, or an out-of-the-way clearing, furnish and use it as a private retreat—for reading, bird-watching, sketching, or tea—whenever weather permits.

ABOVE: A glade lost deep in a woodland garden is the perfect spot for quiet repose or close observation of any small inhabitants who might venture into the dappled light.

ABOVE LEFT: Espaliered fruit trees flank the entry to a wonderful green room, carpeted with lawn, walled with shrubbery, and overhung with leafy boughs. A table and chairs tucked at one end suggest open-air dining and private conversation.

OPPOSITE: Here, sitting picturesquely, a solitary chair is nearly lost amid masses of purple and green. While this bower will provide a summer-long shady retreat, it is in full and fragrant glory while the wisteria blooms overhead.

AS A RESPITE

While garden seats are often placed to take advantage of some landscape feature, you might have a more prosaic reason for siting one: you may simply need a place to rest when gardening. If you spend a lot of time tending your landscape or if your terrain is rough or hilly, then place a bench where it can offset your labor.

ABOVE & RIGHT: This combination cold frame and bench may be the ultimate in raised-bed gardening. It is convenient, practical, and attractive, and anyone with basic carpentry skills should be able to customize something similar.

OPPOSITE: Too much sun can be just as debilitating to the gardener as too much bending, pulling, or digging. If you've no room for a gazebo or pergola, you might consider a covered bench. A basket shelter such as this can also be moved to face away from the sun as needed.

ABOVE: Here, a more formal covered chair is like a tiny garden house, providing shelter from the sun or a gentle rain.

RIGHT: If a long stairway or steep path leads from one part of your yard to another, a bench situated along the way will let you catch your breath. On man-made stairs, repeat the building material for the bench; if you'll be climbing a natural path, you might prefer a fallen log or something more organically shaped.

ON A DECK OR TERRACE

If you have a deck or terrace in your garden, there are several factors that will influence the seating you choose. Is the terrace frequently used as an outdoor living or dining room? Does it focus on a view or border a pool? Is it adjacent to the house? Is it partially walled or covered or approached by steps? Are there potted plants or garden beds on it, or is the landscaping only on the perimeter? The seats and benches that make your terrace comfortable should complement as many of these factors as are present, so keep them in mind as you consider whether the seating should be wood, stone, or metal, movable or built-in, formal or naturalistic.

ABOVE: Slab-sided walls frame the shady terrace adjacent to this cottage. The benches that flank the wonderful potted hydrangea are of fittingly simple slab construction; they quietly welcome and offer rest.

LEFT: This walled terrace with its terra-cotta pavement and interior wood framing gives the appearance of an open-air home. Indeed, the residents use it that way whenever possible, dining and relaxing within the small "rooms."

ABOVE: Here, rustic twig armchairs seem at home under the twisted branches above and are easy to move about to take advantage of the fountain or the view through the gateway.

ABOVE: This marvelous tiled terrace sits like a small stage in lush green shrubbery. Tiled benches were built formally along the sides, but they are too far apart for easy conversation and must be supplemented with other chairs.

ABOVE: Backless stone benches are the perfect choice for this flagstone terrace, where they blend with the low wall, pavement, and tree trunk and allow you turn your gaze and face any direction you please.

OPPOSITE: Here, a perennial border provides a homey sense of place to a small deck perched on the edge of open countryside. Although the vantage point is spectacular, the rustic twig benches seem to grow easily out of the simple weathered planking; the overall effect is natural and unaffected.

SITTING IN STYLE

he design of a seat or bench completes the mood of a garden; its shape and material establish character, which will intrude, subtly or otherwise, upon the setting. The styles of garden furnishings are practically endless, ranging from straightforward, prosaic, and elegant to imaginative, charming, and whimsical. Many designs are traditional and are available in high-quality reproductions from specialty vendors, and most new garden furniture is made from durable—though not necessarily maintenance-free—materials.

Do consider seating comfort—neither charm nor elegance is synonymous with ease. Most garden seats are uncushioned so that they will be weatherproof; if you want the comfort of padding, be sure that cushions will look appropriate on the style of seat you choose, and be prepared to keep them out of the rain. In addition to deciding the style of your garden seating, you will also need to consider the size of each piece (single, double, or greater occupancy) and whether built-in or freestanding furnishings best suit your needs.

FREESTANDING SEATS

Freestanding seats and benches can be moved about as your needs change, but if you plan to move them frequently, be sure to consider their weight. Perhaps a greater advantage to freestanding seating is that you can purchase it ready-made; built-in seating is usually custom made. While stone furniture is durable enough to place directly on the ground, wood and metal will last longer if you set them on some sort of paving, and a small bed of brick or pebbles placed under the legs will protect them from rot—and keep slender feet from sinking into the earth.

OPPOSITE: Carved stone benches are traditionally associated with Renaissance garden design and are frequently seen in formal gardens. Because stone melds with its setting as it ages, it can be just as suitable in naturalistic gardens. Here, a charming little stool perches like a bit of raised pavement in this casually arranged and planted garden.

ABOVE: Cast iron garden furniture, which first became popular during the Victorian era, is available in all sorts of elegant and fanciful designs that often incorporate naturalistic motifs. Depending upon the particular design and locale, it can look truly sophisticated or charmingly tongue-in-cheek. This chair, with its painted patina, masquerades as an archaic construction of grapevine and acanthus.

ABOVE: The proportions of this gracefully curved wood bench are more massive than they might at first appear, but the bench is quiet, elegant, and serene in a large, open setting.

LEFT: For a discreet offer of repose, tuck a plain bench into a soft summer border. This untreated slab has mellowed through the years to sit unobtrusively on a hillside of blooms.

ABOVE: Even a simple wood bench can have elegant proportions; one such as this is quite straightforward, but the shaped planks give it an unexpected finesse.

LEFT: The wood-and-wrought-iron park bench is a classic, seen with minor variations throughout the Western world. It is at home in almost any situation, becoming more or less conspicuous as the environment varies from open to overgrown. Readily available bistro chairs provide a single-seat alternative to this style of bench, but they are not as comfortable for lounging.

OPPOSITE: Sturdy, slatted wood benches, which are often made of farmed teak, are widely available in a variety of formal and informal designs. Because they are so substantial, they can overpower a delicate or tiny garden, but they will complement an open or expansive setting or a substantial wall or hedge.

ABOVE: Humor need not be out of place in the garden. Here, an old plow has been amusingly transformed into a colorful and sunny bench.

RIGHT: Just as fallen tree trunks beckon woodland strollers to stop and sit, these thoughtfully but roughly hewn seats offer a natural resting spot at the edge of a yard—a charming way to redress a storm-felled tree.

OPPOSITE: Rustic twig furniture is most at home in unpretentious settings. This bench grows easily between the green lawn and a soft swath of blue, its lattice back paying wry homage to a more formal and classic bench design.

ABOVE: Rattan and wicker are good choices for sheltered garden seating, as on the portico next to this lovely kitchen garden—an inviting spot for breakfast or tea. These comfortable chairs are lightweight, making them easy to move out of inclement weather.

RIGHT: Lounge furniture is somehow neither as elegant nor as charming as its upright counterparts, but it may bring you closer to truly enjoying your garden. There is an age-old link between grape arbors and reclining; this garden provides a wonderful setting for an afternoon of relaxation.

BUILT-IN SEATS

If you are considering built-in seating for your garden, let the specifics of the setting guide the design of the furnishings. If your garden is formal, your built-in seating should be formal as well; if the setting is naturalistic, you should work with the elements at hand so your seating appears to have grown along with the vegetation. If you are using fences, arbors, or other architectural embellishments, your benches should repeat or complement their design—or be integral with them; if there are natural features such as rocks, stones, or logs, consider using them as construction material.

ABOVE & RIGHT: In rocky hillside environments, you can take advantage of the terrain by building a bench into a bank of earth and stone, then planting the crevices and allowing the whole to grow into a rock garden.

OPPOSITE: Rough timbers can be used instead of stones to create a naturalistic banquette. This one is stepped along a gently sloping lawn where, over time, it has weathered to harmonize with the rocky hillside behind it.

ABOVE: You need not have the excuse (or the ambition) of a stone wall to build a rustic stone bench. This one sits at the edge of a clearing, charmingly overgrown with ivy and morning glories.

ABOVE: If you are building a stone wall somewhere on your property, incorporate a place to sit at a strategic point. This slab-topped bench has a fern-filled planter at each end.

ABOVE: Brick is often used to trim both formal and informal gardens; it is readily available, inexpensive, and easy to work with. Here, a tailored bench sits at the end of a brick-lined pebbled pathway; it uses a heavy plank for its seat.

RIGHT: In a striking setting, understatement may be the key to a well-designed bench. Here, a grassy hillside rolls down to meet a curving pathway and a simple semicircular bench fills a niche carved where the path turns to enter a wood. The harmony of the repeated curves emphasizes the striking transition in the landscape.

BELOW: This lovely little bench is part of a formal terrace railing. It is nearly as delicate as its freestanding cousins and adds a flourish at the end of the railing.

OPPOSITE: Garden arbors filter the strong light of the sun and offer a bit of privacy, making them likely spots for lingering. Benches built inside will always be enticing, and this one, the focal point at one end of a clearing, features high-backed deep-set benches for extra seclusion.

ABOVE: Working gardeners as well as strollers need a place to rest. If you have permanent raised beds in your kitchen garden, think of rimming them with simple plank benches—planting, weeding, and harvesting will be easier. Be sure the benches are steady enough to walk on, so that you'll be able to spade and hoe without fear of tipping over.

SWINGS AND HAMMOCKS

Who can resist the gentle rocking of a hammock or the idle swaying of a garden swing? In daylight or moonbeam, you can escape, dally, linger, or forget, lulled by their drowsy passage, back and forth or side to side, to nowhere.

TOP: A shade-blessed hammock with an eye toward a beautiful landscape is a great reward for hours of dirt-intensive labor. If your garden is as lush as this one, you should relax and revel in the view.

ABOVE: Discovering that two mature trees are the perfect distance apart can easily create an urge to indulge in some fresh-air repose. Should you wish to dress the set, you might embellish the trunks with boxes of flowers when you string up the hammock.

ABOVE: A classic porch swing will give as much pleasure under a tree as on a veranda. Pick a tree with a sturdy overhanging branch, and then enjoy its cool shade in summer and the warm sun in spring and autumn.

LEFT: A high branch, two strong cables, a smooth plank seat, and a good clear lawn are all the young-at-heart need to send fancy flying. Unless you are truly too sedate to indulge in an occasional moment on a swing, be sure that any single-seater you install is broad enough and strong enough to give you—and not just a child—a boost.

CONSIDERING SHAPE,
COLOR, AND PROPORTION

*A*s you choose seating for your garden, your first thoughts will probably be about location and style, but shape, color, and proportion also influence the success with which a bench or chair sits in its environment. You select plants for the way their colors contrast or harmonize and their shapes create line and texture, and you should select garden furnishings with the same thoughts in mind. You may get the most use from your garden seats when the days are at their longest, but you will very likely look upon them all year long, so as you choose them, don't neglect to consider the changing seasons and the way the balance of shape, color, and proportion will be altered as the foliage comes and goes around them.

Green, white, and occasionally black are the classic color choices to impose on garden furnishings. Otherwise, wood, stone, and some metals can be sealed for protection or left to weather naturally. Bright colors may look wonderful in the right spot, but they are attention grabbers. The scale of your bench will be maximized or minimized by the contrast or intensity of its color against its setting—a heavy bench painted white will probably appear more important than the same bench painted dark green.

ABOVE: A park bench placed on a strip of lawn contrasts with a swath of brilliant spring colors, but because the bench is delicate and there is so much green around, the contrast is harmonious. Later in the season, this bench will blend into the bushes.

OPPOSITE: A painted-green bench will harmonize with shrubbery, contrasting gently with the foliage as leaves mature or dapple in the sunlight. This substantial bench stands out just enough to be apparent but does not startle or conflict with the bushes massed around it.

TOP: A white bench set against shrubbery makes a cool but arresting contrast. The formality of this metal settee is emphasized by the grand potted white daisies at each arm.

ABOVE: You might expect to find Mistress Mary tripping lightly down the paths between these small but profusely planted beds, and these fanciful cast-iron seats tucked into the far corner would make a charming resting spot for her.

RIGHT: The green-gray color of this prettily carved bench is an apt choice for this romantic and unusual setting, where it helps the eye make a flowery transition from rock to foliage.

ABOVE: A cast-stone fountain is the focus of this lovely sunken garden, which is paved with tiles made of the same material interspersed with creeping ground covers. The cast-stone bench at the far end is a perfect choice here, and the continuous ecru tone contrasts simply but starkly with the bright color and lush green of the borders—particularly attractive when the warm sun lights the spot.

OPPOSITE: This wonderful little seat seems to have been fashioned by the same hand that shaped the adjacent hedges. The color gray has a cooling effect, particularly when juxtaposed with green, and can be most welcome in warm weather.

ABOVE: Naturally weathered wood tends to gray with age, making it a good choice for a silver-toned garden such as this, where stone paving and blue-green foliage combine to make a monochromatic background that enhances the intensity of the massed lavender blooms.

OPPOSITE: As long as its shape and proportion are appropriate to the landscape, a weathered or clear-finished wood bench is likely to complement any garden. Essentially natural—even though contrived—wood furnishings tend to ride out the changing seasons with grace.

ABOVE: The square lattice back of this small bench is a nice complement to the grid of the brick wall behind it. Although this garden tends to be bleak in the off-season, there is something magical in the way the frost dusts each branch, stalk, and crevice—and the weathered gray of the bench—with silver.

LEFT: Autumn brings a new glory to a wooded garden, showering lawn and furnishings with brilliant color. A substantial wood or stone bench will hold its own in such an expansive setting—whether the season be green, russet, or barren.

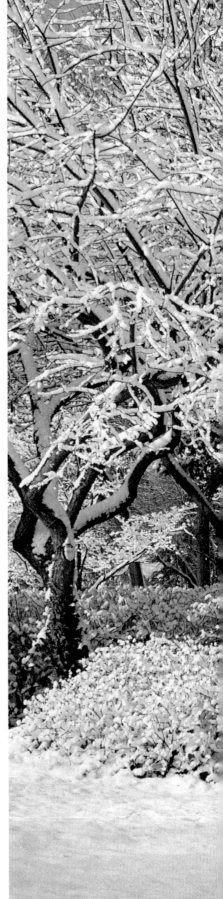

ABOVE & RIGHT: There is nothing like a quilt of pristine snow for transforming a familiar garden into mysterious and larger-than-life scenery. Benches, like bushes and branches, will catch and hold the flakes; the broader and more numerous the surfaces, the more interesting the effect.

Part Four

WALLS AND
FENCES

INTRODUCTION

"*Good fences make good neighbors,*" *wrote Robert Frost. He could easily have said that great fences make great gardens. Gardens truly do love fences—and walls. In fact, the word garden originally meant a walled enclosure.*

The human urge to garden was born out of the desire to build a place of beauty and calm, peaceful introspection, and it was the walls and fences that brought a sense of privacy, peace, and escape. Perhaps now more than ever we need walls and fences in our gardens. They add atmosphere, provide a sense of scale, bring a hint of mystery, and can create order out of nature.

Of course, walls and fences can be nuts-and-bolts practical too. A fence or a wall allows us to mark off an area, create a focus or a vertical viewpoint, block out unwanted views, provide a backdrop for flowers and landscape features, or grow vining and climbing plants.

No matter what the purpose, however, whether it be functional or aesthetic, a wall or fence should be one with the landscape. The secret to incorporating these structures into the existing environment is to utilize materials and designs that will emphasize their ornamental features while masking negative, exclusionary aspects. A wall or fence should stand in harmony with the garden style, the plants, and other structures throughout all four seasons.

Before you dig the first posthole or mix any mortar, it's important to be familiar with your landscape. Is it old-fashioned or modern? Formal or informal? The wall or fence you choose should reflect your garden style in its material and design. Understand the feeling that such materials as stone, brick, wood, and metal bring to the garden. And know that once these building blocks have been stacked, cemented, strapped, or nailed in place, the completed fence or wall will take on a life of its own.

A wall or fence built of the proper material and placed in just the right spot can be the beginning of a great garden or the perfect finishing touch. There's room for one in almost every landscape.
—Warren Schultz

ABOVE: Stone makes a wonderful retaining wall, curving and conforming to the earth as other materials cannot. When built wisely, however, stone walls can do more than hold earth in place; they can also add color, texture, and scale to the garden. Here, the rich, rusty hues of the stones are reflected in the autumn colors of the plants.

OPPOSITE: The urge to peer over this gray, weathered wood gate and fence to catch a glimpse of the enticing pool and hammock beyond is irresistible. Standing outside the gate, a visitor is drawn to the scene. Once inside, the fence offers a sense of security and protection. The rustic post-and-rail design complements the stone patio, while the cascading roses help to soften the edges.

ABOVE: Even when brand-new, a split-rail fence looks as though it sprang from the fields it surrounds. Bringing to mind ranches and farms of a bygone era, a split-rail fence is a fitting choice for a meadow, pasture, or wildflower garden.

OPPOSITE: The approach to this ultramodern house is enhanced and dramatized by these white, seamless walls. The smooth material suits the closely cropped lawn and manicured hedges, while the sharp lines create edges and shadows that play off the bright, gleaming interior of the house.

ABOVE: A stockade fence built with saplings still in their bark jackets replicates the rustic feeling of the frontier fort. When combined with a twig-and-limb bench and moss-covered patio bricks, this fence contributes to a garden scene that feels especially vital.

LEFT: Sometimes a wall seems to exist for the sole purpose of showcasing a plant. This striking combination of adobe and wisteria is an unexpected pleasure; the wall's cracked and weathered face provides a perfect—but untraditional—backdrop for this pendulous plant. And the wisteria returns the favor by smoothing the wall's edges, giving the structure warmth.

ABOVE: Walls can be self-effacing, providing a unifying theme and drawing the eye toward a focal point in the garden. Here, a mortared stone wall creates a curtain behind a formal perennial border, reflecting the sight, discouraging us from gazing out into the distance, and focusing our attention on the flowers. The wall also provides a natural division between the formal, stylized plantings and the wild landscape beyond. Without the wall, the garden would seem abrupt and out of place.

OPPOSITE: With its scalloped top and rolling curves, this adobe wall echoes the hills in the distance as well as maintains congruity with the curving walkway and garden bed. A bench surrounded by adobe-colored ground covers beckons visitors to rest inside this safe haven, separated from the wilds of nature.

OPPOSITE: Iron fences add an old-fashioned elegance to the landscape. Airy and enhanced with decorative flourishes, a wrought-iron fence is also solid and substantial, a perfect support for roses such as this Austrian Copper.

ABOVE: There's room for aesthetics even in the vegetable garden. Perhaps this rustic, colonial twig fence won't keep woodchucks or rabbits out of the greens or lend support to vining crops, but it is an attractive way to keep children and other visitors from straying off the path and trampling the produce.

EARTHWORKS

*S*tone and brick stand alone in the garden, offering what no other material can: a sense of permanence and history. Stone walls are reminiscent of New England, of dappled woods and generations-old farms. Stone makes a warm and friendly fence, conceived not to keep anyone out but only to mark a border or to keep a planting in place. Brick walls hint at older civilizations, bringing to mind the walled Scottish kitchen garden or French parterre.

OPPOSITE: When constructed of large, flat fieldstone, a stone and mortar wall adds a tidy, orderly line to the landscape. Here, an unusual twist has been worked into the design in the form of the planters built along the top. Providing an early splash of color, these primroses can be replaced later in the season to maintain year-round color.

ABOVE: Extreme care and patience are exhibited in this exquisite rock and mortar wall. Such a conscientiously created structure adds much-to-be-admired craftsmanship to a landscape. Considering the different sizes, shapes, and textures of these stones, the plantings should be kept simple and straightforward.

ABOVE: With its ancient and weathered appearance, this field-stone wall looks as if it's been holding back this surging sea of green forever. Highly effective as a retaining wall, this structure proves that there is nothing better than stone for unobtrusively holding earth in place.

OPPOSITE: Fieldstone walls can make their home anywhere. Here, flat, coppery, adobe-like stones carry a hint of the West, and their tumbled-down appearance pairs nicely with the black-eyed Susans that seem to have run wild.

ABOVE: A mortarless wall built of various sized and shaped stones works well in an informal cottage garden. Clearly a wall built for a purpose, these stones support the garden, holding the soil in place and creating a stage for the flowers and herbs.

OPPOSITE: Brick walls, such as this one found at Sissinghurst Castle in England, add a sense of history to the landscape. They present a formal solidity that stone is unable to provide. Bricks are also best for creating the ambience of an outdoor room. Here, gracefully weeping white wisteria is a perfect match for this wall, picking up the burnished white of the bricks.

ABOVE: Although inherently similar in size and shape, bricks can achieve different faces when used in wall construction. This unique pattern creates a brick wall with a lighter, airier feeling. It's perfect for a shady garden, relieving some of the stagnant gloom.

LEFT: Bricks combine beautifully with other materials. Here, a brick wall fades into the background as a bright red wooden door takes center stage.

ABOVE: Although somewhat buried by rockcress and rockrose, this brick wall provides straight, square lines that add a much-needed order to the scene, balancing the mounding wild growth of the creeping plants.

LEFT: A knockout in midwinter, the earthy color of adobe brick provides a beautiful contrast with pure white snow.

OPPOSITE: Strong vertical growers, hollyhocks add visual relief to this adobe wall. In return, the adobe provides a blank canvas that allows the flowers to shine without competition.

THE WARMTH OF WOOD

*W*ood can offer an immediate, easy-to-install change of scene for a landscape. A chameleon in the garden, wood may look rustic and informal or proper and Victorian or quite modern and up-to-date. Wood also works well in a variety of settings because it is available in so many forms, colors, and textures. Further, nothing else can be shaped so easily to fit a garden's mood.

OPPOSITE: Is there anything more American than the split-rail fence? Bringing a stamp of wide-open spaces to the suburbs, a split-rail fence forms a perfect backdrop for a planting of naturalized flowers such as narcissus.

ABOVE: The post-and-rail fence works well for framing a flower garden. The horizontal rails and vertical posts define a negative space that highlights flowers, such as these rudbeckia. The holly-hocks in the background repeat the vertical element of the posts and add depth to the scene.

ABOVE: Nothing beats the friendly welcome extended by a picket fence. This picket-and-wire style carries a refreshing country air, and the full flower heads of the oriental poppies complement the upward stretch of the pickets.

ABOVE: Picket fences can be formal and proper as well. Here, the carved woodwork at the top of the pickets projects a certain artful seriousness. Well-maintained and freshly painted, this fence represents civilization as it holds back the wild roses that appear ready to burst through and overtake the landscape.

OPPOSITE: Picket fences are good choices for showing off plants without obscuring them. Here, this fence's painted white crispness creates an attractive backdrop for plants and draws special attention to the white flowers. In addition, the pickets allow plants to grow up and poke through. The overall look combines well with such garden embellishments as this old-fashioned trellis.

ABOVE: Carrying some of the airy feeling of a picket fence, this woven stockade offers more privacy and protection while avoiding the barricade mentality. The weave allows air and light to pass through, which creates a better growing environment for plants and reduces the incidence of disease. Satisfying both plants and people is key to a good fence.

ABOVE: Bamboo almost guarantees an oriental ambience in the garden. This woven bamboo fence in Kyoto, Japan, establishes a mood of calm and contemplation, which can only be achieved in a garden with a simple design that includes a few select plants, such as this iris, perhaps some water, and plenty of open, neatly raked ground.

OPPOSITE: The best fence provides a sense of place. Made of native aspen wood and complete with ornamental chili pepper ristras, this informal fence evokes a southwestern flavor in no uncertain terms.

OPPOSITE: Commonly called a coyote fence, these strapped-together saplings were used in the western United States to keep marauding canine pests from raiding the henhouse. Because coyote fences recall America's Wild West heritage, informal plantings such as this mass of daisies make good companions.

ABOVE: First and foremost, stockade fences are designed to provide privacy. The trick is to perform that function without seeming antagonistic. This fence pulls it off with a modern alternating-slat design. The whole effect is softened by mounds of daylilies.

ABOVE: Wood fences work best when they are married to the landscape they are built to enclose. Here, this exquisite wooden-slat fence surrounds a patio with matching, custom-made raised beds.

OPPOSITE: A fence, of course, should mirror the style of the structures it surrounds. This ultramodern wooden fence appears to be an extension of the house, while at the same time, it blends with the stark, modern landscape of closely cropped grass. The conifers placed neatly into the niches in the fence soften its edges and mask some of its newness, making the fence look as though the landscape has grown up around it.

WALLS AND FENCES AT WORK

*W*alls and fences can be used simply as garden ornaments and embellishments, structures chosen and put in place because they please the eye. However, walls and fences can be put to work in the garden too. Their uses can range from heavyweight retaining walls to privacy screens to plant trellises. And if they conform to the landscape, these structures can enhance a garden aesthetically while working at the same time.

OPPOSITE: Stone walls allow a gardener to transform an unmanageable hill into a spectacular garden display, such as this peony garden at Naumkeag in Stockbridge, Massachusetts. The overall effect is welcoming, resembling outsize steps leading to the house.

ABOVE: Stone allows a landscaper to change the elevation and slope of an area. Here, what was once a steep and troublesome slope is now a leveled-off lawn, thanks to a stone retaining wall built through the heart of it. The wall makes mowing and maintenance easier, while it also adds visual interest by breaking up the wide expanse of green.

ABOVE: With the wide use of split-rail fences as decorative landscape features, we tend to forget that they were originally invented as working fences to enclose livestock. As insubstantial as they may first appear, split-rail fences can still get the job done. In this pastoral setting, the weeds at the foot of the fence do not detract from the scene; in a more cultivated landscape, however, plantings of perennials or wildflowers at the base of the fence would eliminate the need for mowing between the posts.

ABOVE: In a small suburban backyard, a fence can be essential. This woven stockade fence pulls double duty as it separates the patio from the neighboring yard, creating a secluded retreat and also providing a background and support for plants.

ABOVE: Chain links or barbed wire isn't necessary for keeping a small city garden secure: An attractive wall can easily provide security as well as privacy. Here, a wrought-iron bench running alongside this massive wall beckons visitors to take a moment to relax without fear of intrusion.

LEFT: Sometimes walls and fences are designed to set a scene. Here, a hedge—a living wall—divides a garden into rooms. By hiding the patio with its charming water garden, the hedge serves an important purpose, creating a scene with a delightful element of surprise.

ABOVE: A garden is at its best when it creates a place to escape, a welcome respite from the world of bill collectors and traffic noise. Complete with an inviting bench, this lush green alcove creates a secluded, tension-reducing hideaway.

OPPOSITE: A wall's backbone can be completely invisible, as in the wire frame that supports this ivy. The wire allows latitude for the creative and playful use of vining plants. Here, the greenery creates a private place for reflection, while the peephole frames a scene in the neighboring garden.

ABOVE: Some plants have growth patterns that require support. A fence can serve such a utilitarian function, and it need not be drab or unsightly. Trained to an attractive wooden fence that supports a trellis, the foliage and fruit of these grapevines show their ornamental aspect and can also be easily pruned and harvested so that production is not sacrificed for beauty.

LEFT: Walls can be used to protect plants too. This sturdy brick wall provides a warm and wind-free area for potted plants. The bricks serve as a heat sink, lending some warmth to the tender hydrangeas and sweet peas during cool evenings, while the substantial structure also shelters the top-heavy, trellised plants from strong breezes.

ABOVE: Sometimes a vegetable garden needs a fence that serves as more than just a reminder to stay off the soil. At the height of summer, this simple bamboo trellis will also be the sole support of full-grown tomato and bean plants.

ABOVE: A common design in Great Britain, walled vegetable gardens were originally built for protection not only from small animals but also from poachers and thieves. Although solid stone walls are rarely built for such a purpose these days, they do help to protect tender vegetable plants from harsh weather. The walls store and release a bit of heat, but more importantly, they can also serve as a frost barrier by deflecting cold air.

ABOVE: A stone wall can effectively serve as a gardening space, while at the same time making a spectacular visual statement. In addition to growing trailing plants along the top of the wall, you can often grow small rock-garden or alpine plants in the wall. A bit of peat moss or topsoil pushed in among the stones will get the plants started. Once they begin to grow, they'll energetically carve their own place in the wall, providing a vivid vertical show of blooms.

OPPOSITE: A productive way to grow fruit trees, espaliering requires careful pruning and trellising to a sturdy support. Clinging to this undulating "crinkle-crankle wall," which is a traditional design in some areas of England, these espaliered apple trees are afforded some protection from spring frost that could kill the blossoms.

Walls and Fences
Throughout the Year

Although landscape plantings play a major role in the selection of walls and fences, such influential elements as climate, the native landscape, and the changing aspects of the seasons are also important to keep in mind when selecting materials and styles. Certain designs will add seasonal interest, whereas others will stand out in the off-season when you can't rely on the greens and blooms of plants. During autumn and winter, fences and walls can come to the forefront and add a special signature to the landscape.

OPPOSITE: Framing an arch of blooming fruit trees encircled by narcissus, this simple wooden fence funnels attention down the long stretch of driveway. The eye is drawn to this burst of early spring color, which effectively draws focus away from the rest of the landscape that has yet to bloom.

ABOVE: In an early spring environment, a split-rail fence blends comfortably with its natural surroundings, echoing the bare branches of the trees. Resting in a blanket of newly green grass, this weathered split-rail is at its best rolling through the country-side dotted with trees preparing to bud.

ABOVE: Summer-blooming *Robinia hispida* with burgeoning hosta at its feet beckons visitors through this narrow passage, inviting a stroll between the walls of hedges.

RIGHT: In the height of summer, the lush natural landscape competes with the carefully tended garden. Here, a stone wall helps to shut off background distractions and spotlights a particular area of the garden.

ABOVE: Before the birch and other trees in this scene are in full leaf, the tulips have a chance to snare a good deal of the attention. The bulbs make their colorful contribution raised up in tiered walls that lead the eye to their beds. The undulating shape of the walls is most evident at this time of year, before the greenery and flowers of summer drape over the stones and begin to obscure their form.

ABOVE: When the sun bears down and heat builds up in midsummer, nothing beats a hasty escape to a walled oasis complete with a pool. The planters on top of this wall provide green relief, and as the summer progresses, they will have a chance to grow and tumble over the walls.

RIGHT: The zigzag pattern of this split-rail fence garners attention in autumn. While the lawn loses its luster and flowering plants fade, the autumn foliage shines, and the fence, catching fallen leaves in its nooks and crannies, fits right in.

ABOVE: As autumn leaves begin to fall and create a dramatic coppery carpet, this charcoal gray stone wall comes alive in dark contrast. These boulders would draw little attention in high summer, but here among the golden leaves, both the stones and the stark white gate snap into focus.

OPPOSITE: This combination of an earthy stone wall and post-and-rail fence stands out against the pure white of an early spring snow.

PERFECT PLANTS FOR GROWING UP AND OVER

Walls and fences provide unique opportunities for cultivating plants that need support to flourish. Open the door to the world of climbing, vining, trailing, and clinging plants, and you'll encounter hundreds of annuals and perennials that can be featured for either their foliage or blooms. Plant a few, and they're bound to become prominent features in your garden.

OPPOSITE: With delicate purple or white flowers dangling in large grapelike clusters, wisteria always draws raves. There are several species available: Some are hardy, others are quite fragrant, and still others will produce extraordinarily long flower clusters. The plants are long-lived and grow into stately old friends as the trunks gain girth year after year. Equally at home on a Victorian picket fence or a stone wall, wisteria is, in itself, reason enough to build a wall or put up a fence in the garden.

ABOVE: Old-fashioned, fast-growing, and sure-blooming, morning glories are very reliable climbers in the garden. An annual, a morning glory grows fast and sports flowers in as few as sixty days. A good choice for quick camouflage, these voracious bloomers can obscure a fence that isn't quite up to your aesthetic standards.

ABOVE: Vigorous and very floriferous, trumpet vine climbs and supports itself by means of aerial roots. The plant grows so rapidly and gets so heavy, however, that it sometimes needs additional support and help in hanging on. A midsummer bloomer, trumpet vine can also be trained to grow up and mound over a short fence.

RIGHT: Ivy is so hardy and eager to grow that it can be twisted and pruned and snipped and trained without any worry of damaging it. Here, the plant has been shaped into an intricate design reminiscent of walled gardens in Europe. Pansies growing at the base of the wall provide a splash of spring color.

OPPOSITE: A standard hanger-on, ivy adds stately majesty to plain walls. The plant takes especially well to brick; its aerial roots work their way into every nook and cranny of mortar. Ivy will grow vigorously without much sun, and once it's established, it's very difficult to kill.

ABOVE: Clematis may be the most popular flowering vine in North America, a common sight twining around lampposts on suburban streets. It truly shines, however, when allowed to envelop a fence. An exuberant climber, clematis will bloom profusely as long as it gets full sun and its roots are kept moist and cool.

LEFT: This *Clematis montanum*, also known as anemone clematis, has a unique flower form. Born on slender stalks, the blossoms are often quite large. This Himalaya native is hardy and comes in white, pink, red, or purple.

OPPOSITE: Perfect with bamboo, clematis blooms in a variety of colors. With flowers that can grow as large as dinner plates, clematis adds vibrant color to the garden throughout the summer.

ABOVE: A much-loved garden favorite, roses are available in climbing varieties, which are hard to beat for their masses of blooms and wonderful, sweet fragrance. Climbing roses are often not as hardy as their bush counterparts, however, so be aware of their climatic needs before planting to ensure their winter survival.

OPPOSITE: Roses add an old-fashioned Victorian look to the garden. When combined with a picket fence, that mood is intensified. Whether they are climbers clambering up a wall or fence or vigorous bushes just leaning up against one of these structures, there's no better way to add midsummer color and fragrance to the garden.

ABOVE: Native to the northern United States, honeysuckle doesn't require pampering. In fact, some species are such rampant growers that they have been classified as noxious weeds in certain states. They're still beautiful and fragrant, however, when trained in the garden, such as here where they are growing up a brick wall. Honeysuckles generally prefer full sunshine and will bloom from early spring through summer, depending on the species. Orange is perhaps the most common color, but they also bloom in white, red, pink, and yellow.

OPPOSITE: Tellman honeysuckle is a hardy, deciduous variety. Forming in clusters of eight to twelve, the long bright yellow flowers have buds that show some red.

ABOVE: Chinese jasmine is an exotic climbing plant that lends a touch of the Orient to the landscape. A very tender species, Chinese jasmine is evergreen, providing year-round color perfectly suited to this lattice fence.

RIGHT: When they appear in early spring, the lovely, delicate white, pink, or yellow flowers of Chinese jasmine are exceptionally fragrant.

OPPOSITE: Plants don't always have to be able to climb or cling in order to be at home on a wall. Many small plants will seize an opportunity to grow *in* a wall. Provided with a little root hold filled with soil or peat moss, these lavender plants are quite happy sprouting out of the side of this flagstone wall.

SOURCES

Anderson Design
P.O. Box 4057 C
Bellingham, WA 98227
800-947-7697
Arbors, trellises, gates, and pyramids (Oriental, modern, and traditional style)

Bamboo Fencer
31 Germania Street
Jamaica Plain, Boston, MA 02130
617-524-6137
Bamboo fences

Barlow Tyrie Inc.
1263 Glen Avenue Suite 230
Moorestown, NJ 08057-1139
609-273-7878
Teak wood garden furniture in English garden style

Boston Turning Works
42 Plymouth Street
Boston, MA 02118
617-482-9085
Distinctive wood finials for gates, fenceposts, and balustrades

Brooks Barrel Company
P.O. Box 1056
Department GD25
Cambridge, MD 21613-1046
410-228-0790
Natural-finish pine wooden barrels and planters

Charleston Gardens
61 Queen Street
Charleston, SC 29401
803-723-0252
Fine garden furnishings

Doner Design Inc.
DepartmentG
2175 Beaver Valley Pike
New Providence, PA 17560
717-786-8891
Handcrafted landscape lights (copper)

Florentine Craftsmen Inc.
46-24 28th Street
DepartmentGD
Long Island City, NY 11101
718-937-7632
Garden furniture, ornaments, fountains, and statuary of lead, stone, and bronze

Flower Framers by Jay
671 Wilmer Avenue
Cincinnati, Ohio 45226
Flower boxes

FrenchWyres
P.O. Box 131655
Tyler, TX 75713
903-597-8322
Wire garden furnishings: trellis, urns, cachepots, window boxes, arches, and plant stands

Gardenia
9 Remington Street
Cambridge, MA 02138
1800 685-8866
Birdhouses

Gardensheds
651 Millcross Road
Lancaster, PA 17601
Potting sheds, wood boxes, and larger storage units

Hooks Lattice
7949 Silverton Avenue #903
San Diego, CA 92126
1-800-896-0978
Handcrafted wrought-iron gardenware

Kenneth Lynch & Sons
84 Danbury ROad
P.O. Box 488
WIlton, CT 06897
203-762-8363
Benches, gates, scupture and statuary, planters and urns, topiary, sun-dials, and weathervanes

Kinsman Company
River Road
Department351
Point Pleasant, PA 18950
800-733-4146
European plant supports, pillars, arches trellises, flowerpots, and planters

Lake Creek Garden Features Inc.
P.O. Box 118
Lake City, IA 51449
712-464-8924
Obelisks, plant stands, and gazing, globes and stands

Liteform Designs
P.O. Box 3316
Portland, OR 97208
503-253-1210
Garden lighting: path, bullard, accent, step, and tree fixtures

New Blue Moon Studio
P.O. Box 579
Leavenworth, WA 98826
509-548-4754
Trellises, gates, arbors, and garden furniture

New England Bamboo Company
Box 358
Rockport, MA 01966
508-546-3581

New England Garden Ornaments
P.O. Box 235
38 East Brookfield Road
North Brookfield, MA 01535
508-867-4474
Garden fountains and statuary, planters and urns, antique furniture, sundials, and limestone ornaments

Northwoods Nursery
27368 South Oglesby
Canby, OR 97013
503-266-5432
Nursery features, ornamental trees, shrubs, and vines

Secret Garden
c/o Christine Sibley
15 Waddell Street N.E.
Atlanta, GA 30307
Garden sculpture

Stone Forest
Department G
P.O. Box 2840
Sante Fe, NM 87504
505-986-8883
Hand-carved granite birdbaths, basins, fountains, lanterns, and spheres

Sycamore Creek
P.O. Box 16
Ancram, NY 12502
Handcrafted copper garden furnishings

Tanglewood Conservatories
Silver Spring, MD
Handcrafted period glass houses and atriums

Tidewater Workshop
Oceanville, NJ 08231
800-666-8433
White cedar benches, chairs, swings, and tables

Toscano
17 East Campbell Street
Department G881
Arlington Heights, IL 60005
800-525-1733
Historic garden sculptures, including seraphs and cherubs, and French tapestries

Valcovic Cornell Design
Box 380
Beverly, MA 01915
Trellises and arbor benches (traditional to contemporary style)

Van Bourgondien Bros.
P.O. Box 1000-4691
Babylon, NY 11702-9004
Lilies and lily bulbs

Van Ness Water Gardens
2460 North Euclid
Deptartment 942
Upland, CA 91784-1199
800-205-2425
Water lilies, bog plants, and a variety of plants for water gardens

Vixen Hill Manufacturing Company
Main Street
Elverson, PA 19520
800-423-2766
Cedar gazebos and screened garden houses
Wayside Gardens
1 Garden Lane
Hodges, SC 29695-0001
Worldwide ornamental garden plants and hardy bulbs

Weatherend Estate Furniture
6 Gordon Drive
Rockland, ME 04841
800-456-6483
Heirloom-quality garden furniture

Wood Classics
Box 96G0410
Gardiner, NY 12525
914-255-5651
Garden benches, swings, chairs and tables, rockers, lounges, and umbrellas (all teak and mahogany outdoor furniture)

Australia

Country Farm Perennials
RSD Laings Road
Nayook VIC 3821

Cox's Nursery
RMB 216 Oaks Road
Thrilmere NSW 2572

Honeysuckle Cottage Nursery
Lot 35 Bowen Mountain Road
Bowen Mountain via Grosevale NSW 2753

Swan Bros Pty Ltd
490 Galston Road
Dural NSW 2158

Canada

Corn Hill Nursery Ltd.
RR 5
Petitcodiac NB EOA 2HO

Ferncliff Gardens
SS 1
Mission, British Columbia
V2V 5V6

McFayden Seed Co. Ltd.
Box 1800
Brandon, Manitoba
R7A 6N4

Stirling Perennials
RR 1
Morpeth, Ontario

PHOTOGRAPHY CREDITS

©**Cathy Wilkinson Barash**: p. 141 right

©**Philip Beaurline**: pp. 29, 43, 62 bottom, 76, 77, 96 bottom, 114, 216, 219

©**Hanson Carroll**: pp. 250

©**Crandall & Crandall Photography**: pp. 253, 257, 263, 271, 272 bottom, 281 bottom

©**Rosalind Creasy**: pp. 138 bottom, 140, 143, 144

©**Alan Detrick**: pp. 46 right, 225

©**Ken Druse**: pp. 115 (Design by Ken Druse), 123 right, 150 bottom, 190 left, 194, 200 top

©**Derek Fell**: pp. 139 both, 141 left, 142 both, 153 right, 164, 165, 170 right, 186 left, 187, 193 bottom, 196, 197 top, 210-211 left, 228, 241, 277, 278

©**Richard Fish**: pp. 166, 190 right-191

©**John Glover**: pp. 10-11, 14 right, 17 left, 18 left, 20 left, 24, 27, 28 left, 33, 34, 40, 41 top, 44, 45, 46 left, 48 top, 51 bottom, 55, 58 top, 60 right–61, 73 top, 82 bottom, 88 bottom, 90 right-91, 102, 104 bottom, 118, 119 bottom, 130, Design by The Chelsea Flower Shop: 93 left, 131 bottom, Design by The Chelsea Gardener: 105 top, Design by Daniel Pearson: 93 right, 154, 160, 167 bottom, 172, 176-177 left, 177 right, 180, 186 right, 207, 226, 246, 261, 262, 265

©**Mick Hales**: pp. 106 (Design by Ryan Gainey), 153 left, 184-185 left

©**Saxon Holt**: pp. 161, 162, 174 right-175, 179, 204 right-205

©**Bruce Jenkins/ Full Frame Photo Library**: pp. 152, 181, 188, 189 bottom, 192, 197 bottom, 198, 199, 221

©**Stanley Joseph**: p. 259

©**Dency Kane**: pp. 28 right, 36, 39 bottom, 41 bottom, 62 top, 66 bottom

©**Lynn Karlin**: pp. 201 top, 218, 222, 230

©**Balthazar Korab**: pp. 65 left, 71

©**image/Dennis Krukowski**: pp. 26, 37

©**Michael Landis**: pp. 227, 247, 267 left

©**Michael Lewis**: pp. 173 both

©**Mariane Majerus**: pp. 150 top, 156-157 left, 168, 170 left

©**Charles Mann**: pp. 7, 17 right, 18 right, 19, 20 right-21, 22 both, 23 both, 25, 31, 32 bottom, 35 top, 38 both, 39 top, 48 bottom, 49, 56, 57 both, 58 bottom, 59, 60 left, 63, 64, 65 left, 72, 73 bottom, 74, 75 both, 100 bottom, 103 left, 104 top, 116 bottom, 155, 157 right, 178, 204 bottom

©**Clive Nichols**: pp. 8, 12, 13, 14 left, 15, 16, 30, 32 top, 35 bottom, 42, 47, 50, 51 top, 52, 53, 54, 66 top, 67, 68, 69, 70 left, 80 (Design by Jo Passmore), 81 (Design by David Hicks), 83 (Design by Joan Murdy), 84 left, 85, 86, 88 top, 89, 90 left, 95, 97, 98, 99 right, 105 bottom, 108 left (Design by Lucy Huntington), 108 right, 109, 110, 111 left (Design by Nigel Colborn), 113 (Design by Thomasina Tarling), 117, 119 top, 120 (Design by Beth Chatto), 121, 122-123 left, 124 top, 126, 127, 128 both, 132, 135, 148, 159, 163, 171, 174 left, 183, 185 right, 202, 203, 204 top, 206, 209, 210, Design by Jill Billington: pp.124 bottom, 125, Design by C. Cordy: pp. 84 right, 131 top, Design by Anthony Noel: pp. 87, 92, 94, 99 left, 100 top, 101, 111 right, 112, Design by Daniel Pearson: pp. 96 top, 137, Design by the Old School House: pp. 82 top, 129

©**Jerry Pavia**: pp. 70 right, 116 top, 151, 154, 158, 167 top, 182, 189 top, 194, 195, 208

Photo Nats: ©**Priscilla Connell**: pp. 134, ©**Photo Nats**: pp. 136 left, 138 top

©**Tim Street-Porter**: p. 107 (Design by Annie Kelly - Courtyard "Villa Villambrosa," L.A.)

©**judywhite**: pp. 133, 145, 248, 249, 267 right, 268, 269

©**Cynthia Woodyard**: pp. 193 top, 200 bottom, 201 bottom